OECD Guidelines for Multinational Enterprises on Responsible Business Conduct

OECD
BETTER POLICIES FOR BETTER LIVES

The 2023 amendments to the Guidelines for Multinational Enterprises on Responsible Business Conduct were adopted by the Adherents to the Declaration on International Investment and Multinational Enterprises [OECD/LEGAL/0144]. The Decision on the Guidelines for Multinational Enterprises on Responsible Business Conduct [OECD/LEGAL/0307] was adopted by the OECD Council at Ministerial Level. The Commentaries on both were approved by the OECD Investment Committee. The Foreword is published under the responsibility of the Secretary-General of the OECD and does not necessarily reflect the official views of OECD Member countries.

Please cite this publication as:
OECD (2023), *OECD Guidelines for Multinational Enterprises on Responsible Business Conduct*, OECD Publishing, Paris, https://doi.org/10.1787/81f92357-en.

ISBN 978-92-64-60598-5 (print)
ISBN 978-92-64-81363-2 (pdf)

Corrigenda to OECD publications may be found on line at: www.oecd.org/about/publishing/corrigenda.htm.

Foreword

The OECD *Guidelines for Multinational Enterprises on Responsible Business Conduct* (the *Guidelines*) are recommendations jointly addressed by governments to multinational enterprises to enhance the business contribution to sustainable development and address adverse impacts associated with business activities on people, planet, and society. The *Guidelines* are supported by a unique implementation mechanism, the National Contact Points for Responsible Business Conduct (NCPs), established by governments to further the effectiveness of the *Guidelines*.

Since their introduction in 1976, the *Guidelines* have been continuously updated to remain fit for purpose in light of societal challenges and the evolving context for international business. The 2023 update reflects a decade of experience since their last review in 2011 and responds to urgent social, environmental, and technological priorities facing societies and businesses. Key updates include:

- Recommendations for enterprises to align with internationally agreed goals on climate change and biodiversity
- Inclusion of due diligence expectations on the development, financing, sale, licensing, trade and use of technology, including gathering and using data
- Recommendations on how enterprises are expected to conduct due diligence on impacts and business relationships related to the use of their products and services
- Better protection for at-risk persons and groups including those who raise concerns regarding the conduct of businesses
- Updated recommendations on disclosure of responsible business conduct information
- Expanded due diligence recommendations to all forms of corruption
- Recommendations for enterprises to ensure lobbying activities are consistent with the *Guidelines*
- Strengthened procedures to ensure the visibility, effectiveness, and functional equivalence of National Contact Points for Responsible Business Conduct

The update was conducted by the 51 Adherents to the OECD Declaration on International Investment and Multinational Enterprises and the European Union who participate in the OECD Working Party on Responsible Business Conduct and the OECD Investment Committee. The update benefitted from close involvement of the institutional stakeholders Business at OECD, the Trade Union Advisory Committee to the OECD, and OECD Watch, representing the views of millions of businesses, workers, and civil society members globally. The process also included two public consultations open to interested stakeholders from across the world.

OECD bodies and their respective Secretariats were consulted and contributed to the revisions of thematic chapters of the *Guidelines*, including the Competition Committee; the Committee on Consumer Policy; the Corporate Governance Committee; the Development Assistance Committee; the Committee on Digital Economy Policy; the Employment, Labour and Social Affairs Committee; the Environmental Policy Committee; the Committee on Financial Markets; the Committee on Fiscal Affairs; the Committee on Industry, Innovation and Entrepreneurship; the Insurance and Private Pensions Committee; the Committee for Scientific and Technological Policy; the Committee on SMEs and Entrepreneurship; the Trade Committee; the Working Group on Bribery in International Business Transactions; and the Working Party of Senior Public Integrity Officials.

The update was supported throughout by the OECD Centre for Responsible Business Conduct in the Directorate for Financial and Enterprise Affairs.

Table of contents

Follow OECD Publications on:

- https://twitter.com/OECD
- https://www.facebook.com/theOECD
- https://www.linkedin.com/company/organisation-eco-cooperation-development-organisation-cooperation-developpement-eco/
- https://www.youtube.com/user/OECDiLibrary
- https://www.oecd.org/newsletters/

Declaration on International Investment and Multinational Enterprises

ADHERING GOVERNMENTS[1]

CONSIDERING:

- That international investment is of major importance to the world economy, and has considerably contributed to the development of their countries;
- That multinational enterprises play an important role in this investment process;
- That international co-operation can improve the foreign investment climate, encourage the positive contribution which multinational enterprises can make to economic, social and environmental progress, and minimise and resolve difficulties which may arise from their operations;
- That the benefits of international co-operation are enhanced by addressing issues relating to international investment and multinational enterprises through a balanced framework of inter-related instruments;

DECLARE:

Guidelines for Multinational Enterprises

I. That they jointly recommend to multinational enterprises operating in or from their territories the observance of the Guidelines, set forth in Annex 1 hereto[2], having regard to the considerations and understandings that are set out in the Preface and are an integral part of them;

National Treatment

II. 1. That adhering governments should, consistent with their needs to maintain public order, to protect their essential security interests and to fulfil commitments relating to international peace and security, accord to enterprises operating in their territories and owned or controlled directly or indirectly by nationals

[1] As of 8 June 2023, all OECD Members are Adherents, as well as Argentina, Brazil, Bulgaria, Croatia, Egypt, Jordan, Kazakhstan, Morocco, Peru, Romania, Tunisia, Ukraine and Uruguay. The European Community has been invited to associate itself with the section on National Treatment on matters falling within its competence.

[2] The text of the *Guidelines for Multinational Enterprises on Responsible Business Conduct* is reproduced in Part I of this publication.

of another adhering government (hereinafter referred to as "Foreign-Controlled Enterprises") treatment under their laws, regulations and administrative practices, consistent with international law and no less favourable than that accorded in like situations to domestic enterprises (hereinafter referred to as "National Treatment");

2. That adhering governments will consider applying "National Treatment" in respect of countries other than adhering governments;

3. That adhering governments will endeavour to ensure that their territorial subdivisions apply "National Treatment";

4. That this Declaration does not deal with the right of adhering governments to regulate the entry of foreign investment or the conditions of establishment of foreign enterprises;

Conflicting Requirements

III. That they will co-operate with a view to avoiding or minimising the imposition of conflicting requirements on multinational enterprises and that they will take into account the general considerations and practical approaches as set forth in Annex 2 hereto.[3]

International Investment Incentives and Disincentives

IV. 1. That they recognise the need to strengthen their co-operation in the field of international direct investment;

2. That they thus recognise the need to give due weight to the interests of adhering governments affected by specific laws, regulations and administrative practices in this field (hereinafter called "measures") providing official incentives and disincentives to international direct investment;

3. That adhering governments will endeavour to make such measures as transparent as possible, so that their importance and purpose can be ascertained and that information on them can be readily available;

Consultation Procedures

V. That they are prepared to consult one another on the above matters in conformity with the relevant Decisions of the Council;

Review

VI. That they will review the above matters periodically with a view to improving the effectiveness of international economic co-operation among adhering governments on issues relating to international investment and multinational enterprises.

[3] Annex 2 can be found in the full version of the Declaration on International Investment and Multinational Enterprises, available here: https://legalinstruments.oecd.org/en/instruments/OECD-LEGAL-0144.

Part I: OECD Guidelines for Multinational Enterprises on Responsible Business Conduct

Text and Commentary

Preface

1. The OECD *Guidelines for Multinational Enterprises on Responsible Business Conduct* (the *Guidelines*) are recommendations addressed by governments to multinational enterprises. The common aim of the Adherents to the *Guidelines* is to encourage the positive contributions enterprises can make to economic, environmental, and social progress and to minimise the adverse impacts on the matters covered by the *Guidelines* that may be associated with an enterprise's operations, products and services. Responsible business conduct can enable the creation of a level playing field across global markets, foster a dynamic and well-functioning business sector, and enhance the business contribution to sustainable development outcomes, including solutions to address and respond to climate change.

2. The *Guidelines* are part of the OECD *Declaration on International Investment and Multinational Enterprises [OECD/LEGAL/0144]*. The Adherents to the *Guidelines* make a binding commitment to further their effectiveness in accordance with the *Decision of the Council on the OECD Guidelines for Multinational Enterprises on Responsible Business Conduct [OECD/LEGAL/0307]*. National Contact Points for Responsible Business Conduct play a central role in this regard.

3. The *Guidelines* are intended to encourage responsible trade and investment and thereby multiply the benefits of trade and investment through continuous engagement and improvement in all markets of the world. International trade and investment strengthen and deepen ties between countries and regions of the world and generate substantial benefits that are needed for societies to achieve sustainable development outcomes, including the creation of more and better jobs, skills development, provision of products and services that improve living standards, and access to finance and technology needed for the digital and green transitions.

4. The *Guidelines* express the shared expectation of the Adherents for responsible business conduct of enterprises operating in or from their countries and provide an authoritative point of reference for enterprises and for other stakeholders. They recommend that enterprises undertake risk-based due diligence to identify, prevent, mitigate and account for how they address actual and potential adverse impacts on matters covered by the *Guidelines*. In this regard, the *Guidelines* both complement and reinforce private and public efforts to define and implement responsible business conduct.

5. The *Guidelines* provide voluntary principles and standards for responsible business conduct consistent with applicable laws and internationally recognised standards. Matters covered by the *Guidelines* may be the subject of domestic law and international commitments. The *Guidelines* outline recommendations on responsible business conduct that may go beyond what enterprises are legally required to comply with. The recommendation from governments that enterprises observe the *Guidelines* is distinct from matters of legal liability and enforcement.

6. The ability of multinational enterprises to promote sustainable development is greatly enhanced when trade and investment are conducted in a context of open, competitive and appropriately regulated markets with rule of law and protection of civic space. Governments have an important role to play in supporting effective implementation of the *Guidelines*, including by creating an enabling policy environment to drive, support, and promote responsible business practices. Policy coherence at the national and international level can foster alignment and harmonisation of responsible business conduct initiatives. A smart mix of government approaches and measures, which may include mandatory as well as voluntary

approaches and capacity building and other accompanying measures, is relevant in this regard. The design of specific policies, legislation and other measures on responsible business conduct will be shaped by individual countries' political, administrative, and legal contexts.

7. The political, economic, environmental, social, physical and technological environment for international business is undergoing far-reaching and rapid change. The *Guidelines* themselves have evolved to reflect these changes. In the past decades, international trade and finance has grown significantly as a share of the global economy. Large enterprises still account for a major share of international trade and investment, while cross-border trade and investment by small- and medium-sized enterprises has also increased and these enterprises now play a significant role in international markets. Multinational enterprises, like their domestic counterparts, have evolved to encompass a broader range of business arrangements and organisational forms. Technological developments as well as strategic alliances and closer relations with suppliers and contractors tend to blur the boundaries of the enterprise. The rapid evolution in the structure of multinational enterprises is also reflected in their operations in emerging and developing economies, whose share of cross-border trade and investment is growing. In emerging and developing economies, multinational enterprises have diversified beyond primary production and extractive industries into manufacturing, assembly, domestic market development and services.

8. The nature, scope and speed of economic changes have presented new strategic challenges for enterprises and their stakeholders. Competitive forces are intense and multinational enterprises face a variety of legal, social and regulatory settings. Many multinational enterprises have demonstrated that respect for high standards of business conduct goes hand in hand with growth and profitability. Enterprises increasingly implement business models that pursue sustainable development and support coherence between economic, environmental and social objectives. Enterprises have also promoted social dialogue on what constitutes responsible business conduct and have worked with stakeholders, including in the context of multi-stakeholder initiatives, to develop guidance for responsible business conduct.

9. The adoption of the *Guidelines* in 1976, and their subsequent updates, reflect increased demand on business to follow principles and standards on responsible business conduct. The beginnings of this development can be dated to the work of the International Labour Organisation in the early twentieth century. The adoption by the United Nations in 1948 of the Universal Declaration of Human Rights was another landmark event. It was followed by the ongoing development of standards relevant for many areas of responsible business conduct. The OECD has contributed in important ways to this process through the development of standards covering such areas as the environment, the fight against corruption, consumer interests, corporate governance, science, technology and innovation, and taxation.

10. The *Guidelines* remain the leading international instrument on responsible business conduct. The Adherents to the *Guidelines* are committed to co-operating with each other and with other governments to further their implementation in partnership with the many businesses, trade unions and other non-governmental organisations that are working in their own ways toward the same end.

I. Concepts and Principles

1. The *Guidelines* are recommendations jointly addressed by governments to multinational enterprises. They provide principles and standards of good practice consistent with applicable laws and internationally recognised standards. Observance of the *Guidelines* by enterprises is voluntary and not legally enforceable. Nevertheless, some matters covered by the *Guidelines* may also be regulated by national law or international commitments.
2. Obeying domestic laws is the first obligation of enterprises. The *Guidelines* are not a substitute for, nor should they be considered to, override domestic law and regulation. Failure of governments to uphold the principles and standards consistent with the *Guidelines* or their associated international commitments does not diminish the expectation that enterprises observe the *Guidelines*. While the *Guidelines* extend beyond the law in many cases, they should not and are not intended to place an enterprise in situations where it faces conflicting requirements. However, in countries where domestic laws and regulations conflict with the principles and standards of the *Guidelines*, enterprises should seek ways to honour such principles and standards to the fullest extent which does not place them in violation of domestic law.
3. Since the operations of multinational enterprises extend throughout the world, international co-operation in this field should extend to all countries. Adherents to the *Guidelines* encourage the enterprises operating in or from their territories to observe the *Guidelines* wherever they operate, while taking into account the particular circumstances of each host country.
4. A precise definition of multinational enterprises is not required for the purposes of the *Guidelines*. While the *Guidelines* allow for a broad approach in identifying which entities may be considered multinational enterprises for the purposes of the *Guidelines*, the international nature of an enterprise's structure or activities and its commercial form, purpose, or activities are main factors to consider in this regard. These enterprises operate in all sectors of the economy. They usually comprise companies or other entities established in more than one country and so linked that they may co- ordinate their operations in various ways. While one or more of these entities may be able to exercise a significant influence over the activities of other entities in a group, their degree of autonomy within the group may vary widely from one multinational enterprise to another. Ownership may be private, State, or mixed. The *Guidelines* are addressed to all the entities within the multinational enterprise (parent companies and/or local entities). According to the actual distribution of responsibilities among them, the different entities are expected to co-operate and to assist one another to facilitate observance of the *Guidelines*.
5. The *Guidelines* are not aimed at introducing differences of treatment between multinational and domestic enterprises; they reflect good practice for all. Accordingly, multinational and domestic enterprises are subject to the same expectations in respect of their conduct wherever the *Guidelines* are relevant to both.
6. Governments wish to encourage the widest possible observance of the *Guidelines*. While it is acknowledged that small- and medium-sized enterprises may not have the same capacities as larger enterprises, Adherents to the *Guidelines* nevertheless encourage them to observe the *Guidelines'* recommendations to the fullest extent possible.

7. Adherents to the *Guidelines* should not use them for protectionist purposes nor use them in a way that calls into question the comparative advantage of any country where multinational enterprises invest.
8. Governments have the right to prescribe the conditions under which multinational enterprises operate within their jurisdictions, subject to international law. The entities of a multinational enterprise located in various countries are subject to the laws applicable in these countries. When multinational enterprises are subject to conflicting requirements by Adherents or third countries, the governments concerned are encouraged to co-operate in good faith with a view to resolving problems that may arise.
9. Adherents to the *Guidelines* set them forth with the understanding that they will fulfil their responsibilities to treat enterprises equitably and in accordance with international law and with their contractual obligations.
10. The use of appropriate international dispute settlement mechanisms, including arbitration, is encouraged as a means of facilitating the resolution of legal problems arising between enterprises and host country governments.
11. Adherents to the *Guidelines* will implement them and encourage their use. They will establish National Contact Points for Responsible Business Conduct that promote the *Guidelines* and act as a forum for discussion of all matters relating to the *Guidelines*. Adherents will also participate in appropriate review and consultation procedures to address relevant concerns regarding interpretation and implementation of the *Guidelines,* and to maintain their continued relevance in a changing world.

II. General Policies

Enterprises should take fully into account established policies in the countries in which they operate, and consider the views of other stakeholders. In this regard:

A. Enterprises should:

1. Contribute to economic, environmental and social progress with a view to achieving sustainable development.
2. Respect the internationally recognised human rights of those affected by their activities.
3. Encourage local capacity building through close co-operation with the local community, including business interests, as well as developing the enterprise's activities in domestic and foreign markets, consistent with the need for sound commercial practice.
4. Encourage human capital formation, in particular by creating employment opportunities and facilitating training opportunities for employees.
5. Ensure transparency and integrity in lobbying activities, and refrain from seeking or accepting exemptions not contemplated in the statutory or regulatory framework related to human rights, environmental, health, safety, labour, taxation, financial incentives, or other issues.
6. Support and uphold good corporate governance principles and develop and apply good corporate governance practices, including throughout enterprise groups.
7. Develop and apply effective self-regulatory practices and management systems that foster a relationship of confidence and mutual trust between enterprises and the societies in which they operate.
8. Promote awareness of and compliance by workers employed by multinational enterprises with respect to company policies through appropriate dissemination of these policies, including through training programmes.
9. Refrain from discriminatory or disciplinary action or otherwise engaging in reprisals against workers, trade union representatives or other worker representatives who make bona fide reports to management or, as appropriate, to the competent public authorities, on practices that contravene the law, the *Guidelines* or the enterprise's policies.
10. Refrain from and take steps to prevent the use of reprisals, including by entities with which the enterprise has a business relationship, against any persons or groups that may seek to or do investigate or raise concerns regarding actual or potential adverse impacts associated with the enterprise's operations, products or services. This includes promoting an environment in which individuals and groups feel safe to raise concerns and, where relevant, contributing to the remediation of adverse impacts of reprisals when they occur.
11. Carry out risk-based due diligence, for example by incorporating it into their enterprise risk management systems, to identify, prevent and mitigate actual and potential adverse impacts as described in paragraphs 12 and 13, and account for how these impacts are addressed. The nature and extent of due diligence depend on the circumstances of a particular situation.

12. Avoid causing or contributing to adverse impacts on matters covered by the *Guidelines*, through their own activities, and address such impacts when they occur, including through providing for or co-operating in the remediation of adverse impacts.
13. Seek to prevent or mitigate an adverse impact where they have not contributed to that impact, when the impact is nevertheless directly linked to their operations, products or services by a business relationship. This is not intended to shift responsibility from the entity causing an adverse impact to the enterprise with which it has a business relationship.
14. In addition to addressing adverse impacts in relation to matters covered by the *Guidelines*, encourage, where practicable, entities with which an enterprise has a business relationship to apply principles of responsible business conduct compatible with the *Guidelines*.
15. Engage meaningfully with relevant stakeholders or their legitimate representatives as part of carrying out due diligence and in order to provide opportunities for their views to be taken into account with respect to activities that may significantly impact them related to matters covered by the *Guidelines*.
16. Abstain from any improper involvement in political activities.

B. Enterprises are encouraged to:

1. Engage in or support, where appropriate, private or multi-stakeholder initiatives and social dialogue on responsible business conduct, while ensuring that these initiatives take due account of their social and economic effects on developing economies and of existing internationally recognised standards.

Commentary on Chapter II: General Policies

1. The General Policies chapter of the *Guidelines* is the first to contain specific recommendations to enterprises. As such it is important for setting the tone and establishing common fundamental principles for the specific recommendations in subsequent chapters.

2. Enterprises are encouraged to co-operate with governments in the development and implementation of policies and laws. Considering the views of other stakeholders in society, which includes the local community and those adversely affected or potentially adversely affected by their activities as well as business interests, can enrich this process. It is also recognised that governments should be transparent in their dealings with enterprises, and consult with business on these same issues. Enterprises, social partners and other stakeholders, such as civil society organisations and trade unions, should be viewed as partners with government in the development and use of both voluntary and regulatory approaches (of which the *Guidelines* are one element) to policies affecting them.

3. There should not be any contradiction between the activity of multinational enterprises and sustainable development, and the *Guidelines* are meant to foster complementarities in this regard. Indeed, links among economic, social, and environmental progress are a key means for furthering the goal of sustainable development.[1]

4. Chapter IV elaborates on the general human rights recommendation in paragraph A.2.

[1] One of the most broadly accepted definitions of sustainable development from the 1987 World Commission on Environment and Development (the Brundtland Commission) is: "Development that meets the needs of the present without compromising the ability of future generations to meet their own needs". Global goals to eradicate global poverty, protect the planet, and ensure that all people enjoy peace and prosperity are an important reference point in this regard.

5. The *Guidelines* also acknowledge and encourage the contribution that multinational enterprises can make to local capacity building as a result of their activities in local communities. Similarly, the recommendation on human capital formation is an explicit and forward-looking recognition of the contribution to individual human development that multinational enterprises can offer their employees, and encompasses not only hiring practices, but training and other employee development as well. Human capital formation also incorporates the notion of non-discrimination in hiring practices as well as promotion practices, life-long learning and other on-the-job training.

6. Enterprises participate freely in public discourse. When engaging in public advocacy enterprises should take due account of the *Recommendation on Principles for Transparency and Integrity in Lobbying [OECD/LEGAL/0379]* and ensure that their lobbying activities are consistent with their commitments and goals on matters covered by the *Guidelines*. Governments are responsible for establishing a public integrity framework adapted to the risks relating to lobbying of public officials. The *Guidelines* recommend that, in general, enterprises avoid making efforts to secure exemptions not contemplated in the statutory or regulatory framework related to human rights, environmental, health, safety, labour, taxation and financial incentives among other issues, without infringing on an enterprise's right to seek changes in the statutory or regulatory framework. The words "or accepting" also draw attention to the role of the State in offering these exemptions. While this sort of provision has been traditionally directed at governments, it is also of direct relevance to multinational enterprises. Importantly, however, there are instances where specific exemptions from laws or other policies can be consistent with these laws for legitimate public policy reasons. The environment and competition policy chapters provide examples.

7. The *Guidelines* recommend that enterprises apply good corporate governance practices drawn from the *G20/OECD Principles of Corporate Governance [OECD/LEGAL/0413]*. The Principles call for the protection and facilitation of the exercise of shareholder rights, including the equitable treatment of shareholders. Enterprises should respect the rights of stakeholders established by law or through mutual agreements and encourage active co-operation with stakeholders in creating wealth, jobs, and sustainable and resilient enterprises.

8. The Principles call on the board of the parent entity to ensure the strategic guidance of the enterprise, the effective monitoring of management and to be accountable to the enterprise and to the shareholders, while taking into account the interests of stakeholders. In undertaking these responsibilities, the board needs to ensure the integrity of the enterprise's accounting and financial reporting systems, including independent audit, appropriate control systems, in particular, risk management, and financial and operational control, and compliance with the law and relevant standards.

9. The Principles extend to publicly traded companies within enterprise groups, although boards of subsidiary enterprises might have obligations under the law of their jurisdiction of incorporation. Compliance and control systems should extend where possible to these subsidiaries. Furthermore, the board's monitoring of governance includes continuous review of internal structures to ensure clear lines of management accountability throughout the group.

10. State-owned multinational enterprises are subject to the same recommendations as privately-owned enterprises, but public scrutiny is often magnified when a State is the final owner. The *OECD Guidelines on Corporate Governance of State-Owned Enterprises* are a useful and specifically tailored guide for these enterprises and the recommendations they offer could significantly improve governance.

11. Although primary responsibility for improving the legal and institutional regulatory framework lies with governments, there is a strong business case for enterprises to implement good corporate governance.

12. An increasing network of non-governmental self-regulatory instruments and actions address aspects of corporate behaviour and the relationships between business and society. Interesting developments in this regard are being undertaken in the financial sector. Enterprises recognise that their

activities often have social and environmental implications. The institution of self-regulatory practices and management systems and participation in related multi-stakeholder initiatives by enterprises sensitive to reaching these goals – thereby contributing to sustainable development – is an illustration of this. Self-regulatory practices and multi-stakeholder initiatives should be credible and transparent. Where such initiatives are focused on responsible business conduct due diligence, alignment with relevant international standards such as the *Guidelines* can foster greater effectiveness while reducing complexity and cost for businesses engaged in such initiatives. In turn, developing such practices can further constructive relationships between enterprises and the societies in which they operate. Although enterprises can collaborate at an industry or multistakeholder level, they remain individually responsible for ensuring that their due diligence is carried out effectively.

13. Following from effective self-regulatory practices, as a matter of course, enterprises are expected to promote employee awareness of company policies. Safeguards to protect bona fide "whistle-blowing" activities are also recommended, including protection of employees who, in the absence of timely remedial action or in the face of reasonable risk of negative employment action, report practices that contravene the law to the competent public authorities. While of particular relevance to internal controls, ethics and compliance programmes related to anti-corruption, discussed in Chapter VII, and environmental initiatives, such protection is also relevant to other recommendations in the *Guidelines*.

14. Enterprises should take steps to create a space where concerns about adverse impacts related to their activities or the activities of entities with which they have a business relationship can be safely expressed. Refraining from and taking steps to prevent the use of reprisals are important to protecting civic space and to preventing harm to groups and individuals who seek to or do investigate, express or report such concerns. Reprisals include retaliatory or discriminatory actions that are intended to censor, intimidate, harm or silence critics such as threats, reputational smears, slurs, harassment, intimidation, surveillance, strategic lawsuits against public participation, attempts to criminalise lawful activities, physical attacks and killings.

15. For the purposes of the *Guidelines*, due diligence is understood as the process through which enterprises can identify, prevent, mitigate and account for how they address their actual and potential adverse impacts as an integral part of business decision-making and risk management systems. The OECD due Diligence Guidance for Responsible Business Conduct and OECD sector due diligence guidances help enterprises understand and implement due diligence recommendation of the *Guidelines*. They also seek to promote a common understanding among governments and stakeholders on risk-based due diligence for responsible business conduct. To that end, the OECD Due Diligence Guidance for Responsible Business Conduct sets out a due diligence framework that governments have committed to actively support and monitor. It outlines the following measures: 1. embedding responsible business conduct into policies and management systems; 2. identifying and assessing actual and potential adverse impacts associated with the enterprise's operations, products or services; 3. ceasing, preventing and mitigating adverse impacts; 4. tracking implementation and results; 5. communicating how impacts are addressed; and 6. providing for or co-operating in remediation when appropriate. It also suggests practical actions to implement these measures. Not every practical action mentioned in the due diligence guidance will be appropriate for every situation.

16. Due diligence can be included within broader enterprise risk management systems, provided that it goes beyond simply identifying and managing material risks to the enterprise itself, to include the risks of adverse impacts related to matters covered by the *Guidelines*. Potential impacts are to be addressed through prevention or mitigation, while actual impacts are to be addressed through remediation. The *Guidelines* concern those adverse impacts that are either caused or contributed to by the enterprise, or are directly linked to their operations, products or services by a business relationship, as described in paragraphs A.12 and A.13. Due diligence can help enterprises avoid the risk of such adverse impacts. For the purposes of this recommendation, 'contributing to' an adverse impact should be interpreted as a substantial contribution, meaning an activity that causes, facilitates or incentivises another entity to cause

an adverse impact and does not include minor or trivial contributions. An enterprise's relationship to adverse impact is not static. It may change, for example as situations evolve and depending upon the degree to which due diligence and steps taken to address identified risks and impacts decrease the risk of the impacts occurring.

17. The term 'business relationship' includes relationships with business partners, sub-contractors, franchisees, investee companies, clients, and joint venture partners, entities in the supply chain which supply products or services that contribute to the enterprise's own operations, products or services or which receive, license, buy or use products or services from the enterprise, and any other non-State or State entities directly linked to its operations, products or services. Relationships with individual consumers, who are natural persons acting for purposes that are unrelated to a business, commercial, or governmental activity, are not generally considered 'business relationships' under the *Guidelines* although an enterprise can contribute to adverse impacts caused by them. Business relationships include relationships beyond contractual, 'first tier' or immediate relationships. Entities with which an enterprise has a business relationship may or may not be operating in or from Adherents. The ability of an enterprise to identify, prevent and mitigate actual and potential adverse impacts as described in paragraph A.11, may vary across different types of business relationships, as well as due to other factors, including as described in Commentary paragraph 24.

18. The recommendation in paragraph A.11 applies to those matters covered by the *Guidelines* that are related to adverse impacts associated with an enterprise's operations, products and services, The recommendation in paragraph A.11 does not apply to the chapters on Competition and Taxation. Throughout the *Guidelines,* recommendations related to due diligence should be read in line with paragraphs A. 11-13 and related commentary.

19. The nature and extent of due diligence, such as the specific steps to be taken, appropriate to a particular situation will be affected by factors such as the context of an enterprise's operations, the specific recommendations in the *Guidelines*, and should be proportionate to the size of the enterprise, its involvement with an adverse impact and the severity of adverse impacts. In this respect, the measures that an enterprise takes to conduct due diligence should be risk-based, commensurate to the severity and likelihood of the adverse impact and appropriate and proportionate to its context. Where it is not feasible to address all identified impacts at once, an enterprise should prioritise the order in which it takes action based on the severity and likelihood of the adverse impact.

20. The *Guidelines* recognise that it may not be feasible for most enterprises to assess or to engage with all the individual entities with which they have a business relationship. Where enterprises have large numbers of suppliers and other business relationships, they are encouraged to identify general areas where the risk of adverse impacts is most significant and, based on this risk assessment, prioritise these areas for due diligence in line with the measures outlined in Commentary paragraph 19. Risk-based due diligence related to an enterprise's products or services should take into account known or reasonably foreseeable circumstances related to the use of the product or service in accordance with its intended purpose, or under conditions of reasonably foreseeable improper use or misuse, which may give rise to adverse impacts. Specific recommendations for due diligence related to specific issues are provided in the relevant chapters.

21. Where an enterprise causes or may cause an adverse impact, then it should take the necessary steps to cease or prevent that impact.

22. Where an enterprise contributes or may contribute to an adverse impact, then it should take the necessary steps to cease or prevent its contribution and use its leverage to mitigate any remaining impacts to the greatest extent possible. Leverage is considered to exist where the enterprise has the ability to effect change in the wrongful practices of the entity that causes the harm.

23. The *Guidelines* recognise that responsibility should not be shifted from an entity causing an adverse impact to the enterprise with which it has a business relationship. In this respect where an enterprise is directly linked to an adverse impact through a business relationship, but does not cause or contribute to it, it is not responsible for providing remediation, though it may take a role in doing so, but rather for using leverage alone or in co-operation with other entities, to influence the entity causing the adverse impact to prevent, mitigate or remediate that impact. Where an enterprise does not have sufficient leverage, it should consider ways to enhance its leverage. Enterprises can use or increase leverage in a number of ways to influence entities with which it has business relationships, for example, through support, training and capacity building; engagement to urge them to prevent and/or mitigate impacts; building expectations around responsible business conduct and due diligence specifically into commercial contracts such as management contracts, pre-qualification requirements for potential suppliers, voting trusts, and license or franchise agreements; linking business incentives with performance on responsible business conduct; engaging with regulators and policymakers on responsible business conduct issues; communicating the possibility of responsible disengagement if expectations around responsible business conduct are not respected, collaborating with other enterprises (at sectoral, risk or country level) to pool leverage and implementing common standards of responsible business conduct. Other factors relevant to determining the appropriate response to the identified risks include the severity and probability of adverse impacts and how crucial that supplier is to the enterprise.

24. The *Guidelines* recognise that there are practical limitations on the degree of leverage enterprises have or may be able to build to effect change in the behaviour of entities with which they have business relationships. These are related to product and/or service characteristics, the number of suppliers and other business relationships, the structure and complexity of the supply chain, or the nature of a business relationship or adverse impact in question. For example, in some situations once a service is rendered or a product is sold or re-sold, enterprises may have diminished ability to monitor their impacts or exert or build leverage. In such situations making efforts to identify actual and potential impacts and take preventive or mitigating actions may be particularly important prior to and at the point of sale.

25. Appropriate responses with regard to the business relationship may include continuation of the relationship throughout the course of risk mitigation efforts; temporary suspension of the relationship while pursuing ongoing risk mitigation; or, as a last resort, disengagement from a business relationship either after failed attempts at mitigation, or where the enterprise deems mitigation not feasible, or because of the severity of the adverse impact. Where it is possible for enterprises to continue the relationship and demonstrate a realistic prospect of, or actual improvement over time, such an approach will often be preferable to disengagement. The enterprise should also take into account potential social, environmental and economic adverse impacts related to the decision to disengage. When deciding to disengage, enterprises should do so responsibly including by seeking meaningful consultation with relevant stakeholders in a timely manner and where possible, by taking reasonable and appropriate measures to prevent or mitigate adverse impacts related to their disengagement.

26. Enterprises may also engage with suppliers and other entities with which they have business relationships to improve their performance, in co-operation with other stakeholders, including through personnel training and other forms of capacity building, and support the integration of principles of responsible business conduct compatible with the *Guidelines* into their business practices. Engaging with and supporting small- and medium-sized enterprises with which they have business relationships is particularly important in this respect. Where entities with which an enterprise has a business relationship are potentially exposed to conflicting requirements, imposed for example by different buyers or service providers, enterprises are encouraged, with due regard to anti-competitive concerns, to participate in industry-wide collaborative efforts with other enterprises to coordinate due diligence policies and risk management strategies, including through information-sharing.

27. Enterprises are also encouraged to participate in private or multi-stakeholder initiatives and social dialogue on responsible business conduct, such as those undertaken pursuant to the *Decision of the*

Council on the OECD Guidelines for Multinational Enterprises on Responsible Business Conduct, including the Procedures attached to it.

28. Meaningful stakeholder engagement is a key component of the due diligence process. In some cases, stakeholder engagement may also be a right in and of itself. Stakeholder engagement involves interactive processes of engagement with relevant stakeholders, through, for example, meetings, hearings or consultation proceedings. Relevant stakeholders are persons or groups, or their legitimate representatives, who have rights or interests related to the matters covered by the *Guidelines* that are or could be affected by adverse impacts associated with the enterprise's operations, products or services. Enterprises can prioritise the most severely impacted or potentially impacted stakeholders for engagement. The degree of impact on stakeholders may inform the degree of engagement. Meaningful stakeholder engagement refers to ongoing engagement with stakeholders that is two-way, conducted in good faith by the participants on both sides and responsive to stakeholders' views. To ensure stakeholder engagement is meaningful and effective, it is important to ensure that it is timely, accessible, appropriate and safe for stakeholders, and to identify and remove potential barriers to engaging with stakeholders in positions of vulnerability or marginalisation. The OECD Due Diligence Guidance for Responsible Business Conduct and relevant OECD sector specific guidance includes practical support for enterprises on carrying out stakeholder engagement including as part of an enterprise's due diligence process. This engagement is particularly important in the planning and decision-making concerning projects or other activities involving, for example, the intensive use of land or water, which could significantly affect local communities.

29. Finally, it is important to note that self-regulation and other initiatives in a similar vein, including the *Guidelines*, should not unlawfully restrict competition, nor should they be considered a substitute for effective law and regulation by governments. It is understood that multinational enterprises should avoid potential trade or investment distorting effects of codes and self-regulatory practices when they are being developed.

III. Disclosure

1. Enterprises should take into account established disclosure policies in the countries and sectors in which they operate, and consider the views and informational requirements of shareholders and other relevant stakeholders. Enterprises should disclose regular, timely, reliable, clear, complete, accurate and comparable information in sufficient detail on all material matters. This information should be disclosed for the entire enterprise, and, where appropriate, along business lines or geographic areas. Disclosure policies of enterprises should be tailored to the nature, size and location of the enterprise, with due regard taken of costs, business confidentiality and other competitive concerns.

2. Disclosure policies of enterprises should include, but not be limited to, material information on:

a) the financial and operating results of the enterprise;

b) enterprise objectives and sustainability-related information;

c) capital structures, group structures and their control arrangements;

d) major share ownership, including beneficial owners, and voting rights;

e) information about the composition of the board and its members, including their qualifications, the selection process, other enterprise directorships and whether each board member is regarded as independent by the board;

f) remuneration of members of the board and key executives;

g) related party transactions;

h) foreseeable risk factors;

i) governance structures and policies including the extent of compliance with national corporate governance codes or policies and the process by which they are implemented;

j) debt contracts, including the risk of non-compliance with covenants.

3. It is also important that enterprises communicate responsible business conduct information including as part of their responsibility to carry out due diligence. Some of this information may also be material under paragraph 2. Responsible business conduct information can include:

a) value statements or statements of business conduct intended for public disclosure including policies on responsible business conduct issues that articulate the enterprise's commitments to the principles and standards contained in the *Guidelines*, and its plans for implementing due diligence;

b) policies and other codes of conduct to which the enterprise subscribes, their date of adoption and the countries and entities to which such statements apply;

c) information on measures taken to embed policies on responsible business conduct issues into the enterprise's management and oversight bodies;

d) the enterprise's identified areas of significant impacts or risks, the adverse impacts or risks identified, prioritised and assessed, as well as the prioritisation criteria;

e) its performance in relation to the statements in paragraph 3(a) and the codes in paragraph (b) including the actions taken to prevent or mitigate risks or impacts identified in paragraph 3(c) and (d), including where possible estimated timelines and benchmarks for improvement and their outcomes, including the enterprise's provision of or co-operation in any remediation;

f) information on internal audit, risk management and legal compliance systems;

g) information on relationships with workers and other stakeholders;

h) additional information in line with disclosure recommendations on responsible business conduct information provided in Chapters IV and VI.

4. Enterprises should prepare and disclose information in accordance with internationally recognised accounting and disclosure standards, and refrain from publication of insufficient or unclear information. An annual external audit should be conducted by an independent, competent and qualified auditor in accordance with internationally recognised auditing, ethical and independence standards in order to provide reasonable assurance to the board and shareholders that the financial statements are prepared, in all material respects, in accordance with an applicable financial reporting framework. In order to enhance the credibility of responsible business conduct information, enterprises may seek external assurance attestation of such information.

Commentary on Chapter III: Disclosure

30. The purpose of this Chapter is to help build transparency and accountability around the operations of multinational enterprises. Clear and complete information on enterprises is important to a variety of users ranging from shareholders, potential investors and the financial community to other constituencies such as workers, local communities, special interest groups, governments and society at large. To improve public understanding of the structure and activities of enterprises, their corporate policies and performance with respect to environmental, social and governance matters, enterprises should be transparent in their operations and responsive to the public's increasingly sophisticated demands for information.

31. The first set of disclosure recommendations is identical to disclosure items outlined in the *G20/OECD Principles of Corporate Governance* [OECD/LEGAL/0413]. Their related annotations provide further guidance and the recommendations in the *Guidelines* should be construed in relation to them. The first set of disclosure recommendations focus mainly on publicly traded companies and all material matters regarding the enterprise. Material information can be defined as information whose omission or misstatement can reasonably be expected to influence an investor's assessment of an enterprise's value. This would typically include the value, timing and certainty of a company's future cash flows. Material information can also be defined as information that a reasonable investor would consider important in making an investment or voting decision. To the extent that they are deemed applicable in light of the nature, size and location of enterprises, these disclosure recommendations may also be a useful tool to improve corporate governance in non-traded enterprises; for example, privately held or State-owned enterprises. This set of disclosure recommendations calls for regular, timely, reliable, clear, complete, accurate and comparable information in sufficient detail on all material matters regarding the corporation, including the financial situation, performance, sustainability, ownership and governance of the enterprise. Information about board and executive renumeration is also of concern to shareholders, including the link between remuneration and the enterprise's long-term performance, sustainability and resilience. Enterprises are also expected to disclose timely information including material changes on the remuneration policies applied to board members and key executives as well as remuneration levels or amounts on a standardised and comparable basis so that investors can assess the costs and benefits of remuneration plans and the contribution of incentive schemes, such as stock option schemes, to

performance. Material related party transactions and foreseeable risk factors are additional relevant information that should be disclosed.

32. The *Guidelines* include a second set of disclosure recommendations on responsible business conduct information, including the enterprise's actual or potential adverse impacts on people, the environment and society, and related due diligence processes, which may be material to an investor's decision making and which also may be relevant for a broader set of stakeholders, including, workers, worker representatives, local communities and civil society, among others. In the context of disclosure, due diligence processes, as outlined in paragraph 3, can be a useful means by which enterprises can ensure they are effectively identifying and communicating relevant responsible business conduct information in a consistent and credible manner, including information which may be material. In this way due diligence can support enterprises in identifying material risks and impacts, and enhance the relevance, quality and comparability of disclosures under both paragraphs 2 and 3. Furthermore, due diligence processes can be a means of ensuring credible reporting against enterprise goals and commitments for which clearly identifiable or measurable targets may not exist. Several jurisdictions allow or require the consideration of stakeholder interests and many enterprises provide information on a broader set of topics than financial performance, through which they can demonstrate commitment to and performance on responsible business practices more generally. This second type of disclosure – or communication with the public and with other parties directly affected by the enterprise's activities or business relationships – may pertain to entities that extend beyond those covered in the enterprise's financial accounts. For example, it may also cover information on the activities of subcontractors, suppliers, joint venture partners or others with whom the enterprise has a business relationship.

33. The two sets of disclosures in paragraph 2 and paragraph 3 are interrelated and some information may be relevant for both. In order to determine what information should be disclosed under paragraph 2, the *Guidelines* use the concept of materiality. Information under paragraph 2, including related to responsible business conduct issues and due diligence, could also be considered material if information whose omission or misstatement can reasonably be expected to influence an investor's assessment of an enterprise's value, timing and certainty of an enterprise's future cash flows or an investor's investment or voting decisions. The determination of which information is material may vary over time, and according to the local context, enterprise specific circumstances and jurisdictional requirements. Users of financial information and market participants need information on reasonably foreseeable material risks that may include: risks that are specific to the industry or the geographical areas in which the enterprise operates; dependence on commodities and supply chains; financial market risks including interest rate or currency risk; risks related to derivatives and off-balance sheet transactions; business conduct risks; digital security risks; compliance risks; and sustainability risks, notably climate-related risks. Some jurisdictions may also require or recommend disclosing sustainability matters critical to an enterprise's workforce and key stakeholders or an enterprise's influence on non-diversifiable risks.

34. In relation to information disclosed under paragraph 3, risks and impacts that may not seem to be financially material but that are relevant to people, and the planet may be financially material for an enterprise at some point.

35. Disclosure recommendations in this Chapter and throughout the *Guidelines* should not place unreasonable administrative or cost burdens on enterprises. Nor should enterprises be expected to disclose information that may endanger their competitive position unless disclosure is necessary to fully inform an investor's decisions and to avoid misleading investors.

36. Information should be prepared and disclosed in accordance with internationally recognised accounting and disclosure standards. An annual external audit should be conducted by an independent, competent and qualified, auditor in accordance with internationally recognised auditing, ethical and independence standards in order to provide reasonable assurance on whether the financial statements are prepared in all material respects in accordance with an applicable financial reporting framework.

37. Many enterprises have adopted measures designed to help them comply with the law and standards of business conduct, and to enhance the transparency of their operations. A growing number of firms have issued voluntary codes of corporate conduct, which are expressions of commitments to international standards or ethical values in such areas as environment, including climate change, biodiversity, human rights, labour standards, consumer protection, or taxation. Specialised management systems have been or are being developed and continue to evolve with the aim of helping them respect these commitments – these involve information systems, operating procedures and training requirements.

38. Enterprises may be required to report against broader disclosure standards mandated by regulatory or listing authorities and, where consistent with a jurisdiction's legal and disclosure requirements, should seek to adopt and align with emerging global best practice and evolving disclosure standards, for example on climate and emissions. Enterprises are co-operating with NGOs and intergovernmental organisations in developing reporting standards that enhance enterprises' ability to communicate how their activities influence sustainable development outcomes.

39. Enterprises are encouraged to proactively communicate relevant responsible business conduct information, to provide easily accessible, user friendly, timely, accurate, clear, and complete information, to provide economical access to published information and to consider making use of information technologies to meet this goal. Information that is made available to users in home markets should also be available to all interested users with consideration for accessibility. Enterprises should seek to ensure information is presented appropriately for different target audiences and may take special steps to make information available to communities that do not have access to online or printed media (for example, remote or impoverished communities that are directly affected by the enterprise's activities).

40. Review of responsible business conduct information by an independent, competent and qualified entity in accordance with internationally recognised assurance standards can substantiate and enhance confidence in the information disclosed and contribute to higher quality and more comparable reporting.

IV. Human Rights

States have the duty to protect human rights. Enterprises should, within the framework of internationally recognised human rights, the international human rights obligations of the countries in which they operate as well as relevant domestic laws and regulations:

1. Respect human rights, which means they should avoid infringing on the human rights of others and should address adverse human rights impacts with which they are involved.
2. Within the context of their own activities, avoid causing or contributing to adverse human rights impacts and address such impacts when they occur.
3. Seek ways to prevent or mitigate adverse human rights impacts that are directly linked to their business operations, products or services by a business relationship, even if they do not contribute to those impacts.
4. Have a publicly available policy commitment to respect human rights.
5. Carry out human rights due diligence as appropriate to their size, the nature and context of operations and the severity of the risks of adverse human rights impacts.
6. Provide for or co-operate through legitimate processes in the remediation of adverse human rights impacts where they identify that they have caused or contributed to these impacts.

Commentary on Chapter IV: Human Rights

41. This chapter opens with a chapeau that sets out the framework for the specific recommendations concerning enterprises' respect for human rights. It draws upon the United Nations 'Protect, Respect and Remedy Framework for Business and Human Rights' and is in line with the Guiding Principles on Business and Human Rights for its implementation as well as the ILO Tripartite Declaration of Principles concerning Multinational Enterprises and Social Policy.

42. The chapeau and the first paragraph recognise that States have the duty to protect human rights, and that enterprises, regardless of their size, sector, operational context, ownership and structure, should respect human rights wherever they operate. Respect for human rights is the global standard of expected conduct for enterprises independently of States' abilities and/or willingness to fulfil their human rights obligations, and does not diminish those obligations.

43. A State's failure either to enforce relevant domestic laws, or to implement international human rights obligations or the fact that it may act contrary to such laws or international obligations does not diminish the expectation that enterprises respect human rights. In countries where domestic laws and regulations conflict with internationally recognised human rights, enterprises should seek ways to honour them to the fullest extent which does not place them in violation of domestic law, consistent with paragraph 2 of the Chapter on Concepts and Principles.

44. In all cases and irrespective of the country or specific context of enterprises' operations, reference should be made at a minimum to the internationally recognised human rights expressed in the International Bill of Human Rights, consisting of the Universal Declaration of Human Rights and the main instruments through which it has been codified: the International Covenant on Civil and Political Rights and the

International Covenant on Economic, Social and Cultural Rights, and to the principles concerning fundamental rights set out in the International Labour Organisation Declaration on Fundamental Principles and Rights at Work.

45. Enterprises can have an impact on virtually the entire spectrum of internationally recognised human rights. In practice, some human rights may be at greater risk of adverse impacts than others in particular industries or contexts, and therefore will be the focus of heightened attention. However, situations may change, so all rights should be the subject of periodic review. Depending on circumstances, enterprises may need to consider additional standards. For instance, enterprises should respect the human rights of individuals belonging to specific groups or populations that require particular attention, where they may have adverse human rights impacts on them. Enterprises should pay special attention to any particular adverse impacts on individuals, for example human rights defenders, who may be at heightened risk due to marginalisation, vulnerability or other circumstances, individually or as members of certain groups or populations, including Indigenous Peoples. OECD due diligence guidance, including the OECD Due Diligence Guidance on Responsible Business Conduct, the OECD Due Diligence Guidance on Meaningful Stakeholder Engagement in the Extractive Sector, and the OECD-FAO Guidance for Responsible Agricultural Supply Chains provides further practical guidance in this regard, including in relation to Free, Prior and Informed Consent (FPIC). United Nations instruments have elaborated on the rights of Indigenous Peoples (UN Declaration on the Rights of Indigenous Peoples); persons belonging to national or ethnic, religious and linguistic minorities; women; children; persons with disabilities; and migrant workers and their families. Moreover, in situations of armed conflict enterprises should respect the standards of international humanitarian law. In the context of armed conflict or heightened risk of gross abuses, enterprises should conduct enhanced due diligence in relation to adverse impacts, including violations of international humanitarian law.

46. In paragraph 1, addressing actual and potential adverse human rights impacts consists of taking adequate measures for their identification, prevention, where possible, and mitigation of potential human rights impacts, remediation of actual impacts, and accounting for how the adverse human rights impacts are addressed. The term 'infringing' refers to adverse impacts that an enterprise may have on the human rights of individuals.

47. Paragraph 2 recommends that enterprises avoid causing or contributing to adverse human rights impacts through their own activities and address such impacts when they occur. 'Activities' can include both actions and omissions. Where an enterprise causes or may cause an adverse human rights impact, it should take the necessary steps to cease or prevent the impact. Where an enterprise contributes or may contribute to such an impact, it should take the necessary steps to cease or prevent its contribution and use its leverage to mitigate any remaining impact to the greatest extent possible. Leverage is considered to exist where the enterprise has the ability to effect change in the practices of an entity that cause adverse human rights impacts.

48. Paragraph 3 addresses more complex situations where an enterprise has not contributed to an adverse human rights impact, but that impact is nevertheless directly linked to its operations, products or services by its business relationship with another entity. Paragraph 3 is not intended to shift responsibility from the entity causing an adverse human rights impact to the enterprise with which it has a business relationship. Meeting the expectation in paragraph 3 would entail an enterprise, acting alone or in co-operation with other entities, as appropriate, to use and where needed enhance its leverage to influence the entity causing the adverse human rights impact to prevent or mitigate that impact. 'Business relationships' include relationships with business partners, entities in its supply chain, and any other non-State or State entity directly linked to its business operations, products or services. Among the factors that will enter into the determination of the appropriate action in such situations are the enterprise's leverage over the entity concerned, how crucial the relationship is to the enterprise, the severity of the impact, and whether terminating the relationship with the entity itself would have adverse human rights impacts.

49. Paragraph 4 recommends that enterprises express their commitment to respect human rights through a publicly available statement of policy that: *(i)* is approved at the most senior level of the enterprise; *(ii)* is informed by relevant internal and/or external expertise; *(iii)* stipulates the enterprise's human rights expectations of personnel, business partners and other parties directly linked to its operations, products or services; *(iv)* is communicated internally and externally to all personnel, business partners and other relevant parties; *(v)* is reflected in operational policies and procedures necessary to embed it throughout the enterprise.

50. Paragraph 5 recommends that enterprises carry out human rights due diligence. The process entails assessing actual and potential human rights impacts, integrating and acting upon the findings, tracking responses as well as communicating how impacts are addressed. Human rights due diligence can be included within broader enterprise risk management systems, provided that it goes beyond simply identifying and managing material risks to the enterprise itself to include the risks to rights-holders. It is an on-going exercise, recognising that human rights risks may change over time as the enterprise's operations and operating context evolve. Complementary guidance on due diligence, including in relation to supply chains, and appropriate responses to risks arising in supply chains are provided under paragraphs A.11 to A.13 of the Chapter on General Policies and their Commentaries. In addition, further guidance has been developed for specific sectors and risk issues, as well as at a cross-sectoral level through the OECD Due Diligence Guidance on Responsible Business Conduct. Conducting human rights due diligence may involve considering distinct and intersecting risks, including those related to individual characteristics or to vulnerable or marginalised groups. Meaningful stakeholder engagement is important in this regard and considering ways to maximise sustainable development outcomes for such groups may also be relevant.

51. When enterprises identify through their human rights due diligence process or other means that they have caused or contributed to an adverse impact, the *Guidelines* recommend that enterprises provide for or co-operate in their remediation through legitimate processes. Enterprises should establish or participate in processes to enable remediation. Some situations require co-operation with judicial or State-based non-judicial mechanisms. In others, operational-level grievance mechanisms for those potentially impacted by enterprises' activities can be an effective means of providing for such processes when they meet the core criteria of: legitimacy, accessibility, predictability, equitability, compatibility with the *Guidelines,* transparency, rights-compatibility, being a source of continuous learning, and are based on dialogue and engagement with a view to seeking agreed solutions. Such mechanisms can be administered by an enterprise alone or in collaboration with other stakeholders and can be a source of continuous learning. Operational-level grievance mechanisms should not be used to undermine the role of trade unions in addressing labour-related disputes, nor should such mechanisms preclude access to judicial or non-judicial grievance mechanisms, including the National Contact Points under the *Guidelines*.

V. Employment and Industrial Relations

Enterprises should, within the framework of applicable law, regulations and prevailing labour relations and employment practices and applicable international labour standards, avoiding any unlawful employment and industrial relations practices, and in line with due diligence expectations described in Chapters II and IV:

1.

a) Respect the right of workers to establish or join trade unions and representative organisations of their own choosing, including by avoiding interfering with workers' choice to establish or join a trade union or representative organisation of their own choosing.

b) Respect the right of workers to have trade unions and representative organisations of their own choosing recognised for the purpose of collective bargaining, and engage in constructive negotiations, either individually or through employers' associations, with such representatives with a view to reaching agreements on terms and conditions of employment.

c) Contribute to the effective abolition of child labour, and take immediate and effective measures to secure the elimination of the worst forms of child labour as a matter of urgency.

d) Contribute to the elimination of all forms of forced or compulsory labour and take immediate and effective measures towards the elimination of forced or compulsory labour as a matter of urgency.

e) Be guided throughout their operations by the principle of equality of opportunity and treatment in employment and not discriminate against their workers with respect to employment or occupation on such grounds as race, colour, sex, age, religion, political opinion, national extraction or social origin, persons with disabilities or other status, unless selectivity concerning worker characteristics furthers established governmental policies which specifically promote greater equality of employment opportunity or relates to the inherent requirements of a job.

f) Provide a safe and healthy working environment in line with the ILO Declaration on Fundamental Principles and Rights at Work.

2.

a) Provide such facilities to workers' representatives as may be necessary to assist in the development of effective collective agreements.

b) Provide information in a timely manner to workers' representatives which is needed for meaningful negotiations on conditions of employment.

c) Provide information to workers and their representatives which enables them to obtain a true and fair view of the performance of the entity or, where appropriate, the enterprise as a whole.

3. Promote consultation and co-operation between employers and workers and their representatives through legitimate processes, structures or mechanisms on matters of mutual concern.

4.

a) Observe standards of employment, contractual arrangements and industrial relations throughout their operations.

b) When multinational enterprises operate in other countries, wages, benefits and conditions of work offered across their operations should not be less favourable to the workers than those offered by comparable employers in the host country. Where comparable employers may not exist, enterprises should provide the best possible wages, benefits and conditions of work, within the framework of government policies and applicable international standards. These should be related to the economic position of the enterprise, but should be at least adequate to satisfy the basic needs of the workers and their families.

c) Maintain the highest standards of safety and health at work.

5. In their operations, to the greatest extent practicable, employ local workers and provide training with a view to improving skill levels, in co-operation with worker representatives and, where appropriate, relevant governmental authorities.

6. In considering changes in their operations which would have major employment effects, in particular in the case of the closure of an entity involving collective lay-offs or dismissals, provide reasonable notice of such changes to representatives of the affected workers and their organisations, and, where appropriate, to the relevant governmental authorities, and co-operate with the worker representatives and appropriate governmental authorities so as to mitigate to the maximum extent practicable adverse effects of such changes. In light of the specific circumstances of each case, it would be appropriate if management were able to give such notice prior to the final decision being taken. Other means may also be employed to provide meaningful co-operation to mitigate the effects of such decisions.

7. In the context of bona fide negotiations with workers' representatives on conditions of employment, or while workers are exercising a right to organise, not threaten to transfer the whole or part of an operating unit from the country concerned nor transfer workers from the enterprises' component entities in other countries in order to influence unfairly those negotiations or to hinder the exercise of a right to organize or bargain collectively.

8. Enable authorised representatives of the workers in their employment to negotiate on collective bargaining or labour-management relations issues and allow the parties to consult on matters of mutual concern with representatives of management who are authorised to take decisions on these matters.

Commentary on Chapter V: Employment and Industrial Relations

52. This chapter opens with a chapeau that includes a reference to "applicable" law and regulations, which is meant to acknowledge the fact that multinational enterprises, while operating within the jurisdiction of particular countries, may be subject to national and international levels of regulation of employment and industrial relations matters. The terms "prevailing labour relations" and "employment practices" are sufficiently broad to permit a variety of interpretations in light of different national circumstances – for example, different bargaining options provided for workers under national laws and regulations.

53. The International Labour Organisation (ILO) is the competent body to set and deal with international labour standards, and to promote fundamental rights at work as recognised in its Declaration on Fundamental Principles and Rights at Work. The *Guidelines*, as a non-binding instrument, have a role to play in promoting observance of these standards and principles among multinational enterprises. The provisions of the *Guidelines* chapter echo relevant provisions of the Declaration, as well as the ILO Tripartite Declaration of Principles concerning Multinational Enterprises and Social Policy, (the ILO MNE Declaration). The ILO MNE Declaration sets out principles in the fields of employment, training, working conditions, and industrial relations, while the OECD *Guidelines* cover all major aspects of corporate behaviour. The OECD *Guidelines* and the ILO MNE Declaration refer to the behaviour expected from enterprises and are intended to parallel and not conflict with each other. The ILO MNE Declaration can therefore be of use in understanding the *Guidelines* to the extent that it is of a greater degree of elaboration.

However, the responsibilities for the follow-up procedures under the ILO MNE Declaration and the *Guidelines* are institutionally separate.

54. The terminology used in Chapter V is consistent with that used in the ILO MNE Declaration. It is recognised that in the absence of an employment relationship, enterprises are nevertheless expected to act in accordance with the risk-based due diligence and supply chain recommendations in paragraphs A.11 to A.14 of Chapter II on General Policies. This is especially relevant in sectors where informality, short-term working arrangements, decent work deficits and digital transformation may be more common.

55. These recommendations do not interfere with true civil and commercial relationships, but rather seek to ensure that individuals in an employment relationship have the protection that is due to them in the context of the *Guidelines*.

56. Paragraph 1 of this chapter is designed to echo all fundamental principles and rights at work which are contained in the ILO Declaration on Fundamental Principles and Rights at Work, namely the freedom of association and right to collective bargaining, the effective abolition of child labour, the elimination of all forms of forced or compulsory labour, non-discrimination in employment and occupation, and promoting a safe and healthy working environment. These principles and rights have been developed in the form of specific rights and obligations in ILO Conventions recognised as fundamental.

57. Paragraph 1c) recommends that multinational enterprises contribute to the effective abolition of child labour in the sense of the ILO Declaration on Fundamental Principles and Rights at Work. Long-standing ILO instruments on child labour are Convention 138 and Recommendation 146 (both adopted in 1973), concerning minimum ages for employment, and ILO Convention 182 and Recommendation 190 concerning the worst forms of child labour. Through their labour management practices, their creation of high-quality, well-paid, decent work and their contribution to economic growth, multinational enterprises can play a positive role in helping to address the root causes of poverty in general and of child labour in particular. It is important to acknowledge and encourage the role of multinational enterprises in contributing to the search for a lasting solution to the problem of child labour. In this regard, raising the standards of education of children living in host countries is especially noteworthy.

58. Paragraph 1d) recommends that enterprises contribute to the elimination of all forms of forced and compulsory labour, another principle derived from the ILO Declaration on Fundamental Principles and Rights at Work, and recognised as the human right to be free from forced and compulsory labour in the International Covenant on Civil and Political Rights (ICCPR). The reference to this core labour right is based on the ILO Convention 29 of 1930 and its Protocol of 2014 and Convention 105 of 1957. Convention 29 calls on governments to "suppress the use of forced or compulsory labour in all its forms within the shortest possible period", while Convention 105 calls on governments to "suppress and not to make use of any form of forced or compulsory labour" for certain enumerated purposes (for example, as a means of political coercion or labour discipline), and "to take effective measures to secure [its] immediate and complete abolition". At the same time, it is understood that the ILO is the competent body to deal with the difficult issue of prison labour, in particular when it comes to the hiring-out of prisoners to (or their placing at the disposal of) private individuals, enterprises or associations. Enterprises should take the necessary steps to prevent human trafficking, including for the purpose of forced labour, and address coercive means, including debt bondage. Enterprises should respond to indicators set out in the ILO Indicators of Forced Labour and bolster transparency around actions taken to address risks of forced labour associated with their operations, products and services.

59. The reference to the principle of non-discrimination with respect to employment and occupation in paragraph 1e) is considered to apply to such terms and conditions as hiring, job assignment, discharge, pay and benefits, promotion, transfer or relocation, termination, training and retirement. The list of non-permissible grounds for discrimination which is taken from ILO Discrimination (Employment and Occupation) Convention 111, ILO Convention 100, the Maternity Protection Convention 183, Employment (Disabled Persons) Convention 159, the Older Workers Recommendation 162 and the HIV and AIDS at

Work Recommendation 200, considers that any distinction, exclusion or preference on these grounds is in violation of the Conventions, Recommendations and Codes. The term "other status" for the purposes of the *Guidelines* refers to trade union activity and personal characteristics such as age, disability, gender, pregnancy, marital status, sexual orientation, or HIV status. Consistent with the provisions in paragraph 1e), enterprises are expected to promote equal opportunities for all with special emphasis on equal criteria for selection, remuneration, training, and promotion, and equal application of those criteria, and prevent discrimination or dismissals on the grounds of marriage, pregnancy or of those workers with family responsibilities. Relevant in this regard is ILO Convention 190 on Violence and Harassment.

60. Paragraph 1f) recommends all enterprises to provide a safe and healthy working environment, including by preventing accidents and injury to health arising out of, linked with or occurring in the course of work, by minimising, so far as is reasonably practicable, the causes of hazards inherent in the working environment.

61. In paragraph 2c) of this chapter, information provided by enterprises to their workers and their representatives is expected to provide a "true and fair view" of performance. It relates to the following: the structure of the enterprise, its economic and financial situation and prospects, its adverse environmental health and safety impacts, employment trends, and expected substantial changes in operations, taking into account legitimate requirements of business confidentiality. Considerations of business confidentiality may mean that information on certain points may not be provided, or may not be provided without safeguards.

62. The reference to consultative forms of worker participation in paragraph 3 of the Chapter is taken from ILO Recommendation 94 concerning Consultation and Co-operation between Employers and Workers at the Level of the Undertaking. It also conforms to a provision contained in the ILO MNE Declaration. Such consultative arrangements should not substitute for workers' right to bargain over terms and conditions of employment. A recommendation on consultative arrangements with respect to working arrangements is also part of paragraph 8.

63. In paragraph 4, employment and industrial relations standards are understood to include compensation and working-time arrangements. The reference to occupational health and safety implies that multinational enterprises are expected to follow prevailing regulatory standards and industry norms to minimise the risk of accidents and injury to health arising out of, linked with, or occurring in, the course of employment. This encourages enterprises to work to raise the level of performance with respect to occupational health and safety in all parts of their operation even where this may not be formally required by existing regulations in countries in which they operate. It also encourages enterprises to respect workers' ability to remove themselves from a work situation when there is reasonable justification to believe that it presents an imminent and serious risk to health or safety. Reflecting their importance and complementarities among related recommendations, health and safety concerns are echoed elsewhere in the *Guidelines*, most notably in chapters on Consumer Interests and the Environment. The ILO List of Occupational Diseases Recommendation 194 provides an indicative list of occupational diseases as well as codes of practice and guides which can be taken into account by enterprises for implementing this recommendation of the *Guidelines*. Further guidance for enterprises on occupational health and safety is available in Part IV (Action at the level of the undertakings) of ILO Convention on Occupational Safety and Health 155 and the Guidelines on Occupational Safety and Health Management Systems (ILO-OSH).

64. The recommendation in paragraph 5 of the chapter encourages multinational enterprises to recruit an adequate workforce share locally, including managerial personnel, and to provide training to them. Training for up-skilling and re-skilling should anticipate future changes in operations and employer needs, including those responding to societal, environmental technological changes, risks and opportunities linked to automation, digitalisation, just transition and sustainable development. Language in this paragraph on training and skill levels complements the text in paragraph A.4 of the General Policies chapter on encouraging human capital formation. The reference to local workers complements the text encouraging

local capacity building in paragraph A.3 of the General Policies chapter. In accordance with the ILO Human Resources Development Recommendation 195, enterprises are also encouraged to invest, to the greatest extent practicable, in training and lifelong learning while ensuring equal opportunities to training for women and other vulnerable groups, such as youth, low-skilled people, people with disabilities, migrants, older workers, and Indigenous Peoples.

65. Enterprises have an important role to play in promoting and creating decent work. Paragraph 6 recommends that enterprises provide reasonable notice to the representatives of workers and relevant government authorities, of changes in their operations which would have major effects upon the livelihood of their workers, in particular the closure of an entity or moves towards automation involving collective or large-scale layoffs or dismissals. As stated therein, the purpose of this provision is to afford an opportunity for co-operation to mitigate the effects of such changes. This is an important principle that is widely reflected in the industrial relations laws and practices of Adherents, although the approaches taken to ensuring an opportunity for meaningful co-operation are not identical in all adhering countries. The paragraph also notes that it would be appropriate if, in light of specific circumstances, management were able to give such notice prior to the final decision. Indeed, notice prior to the final decision is a feature of industrial relations laws and practices in a number of adhering countries. However, it is not the only means to ensure an opportunity for meaningful co-operation to mitigate the effects of such decisions, and the laws and practices of other Adherents provide for other means such as defined periods during which consultations must be undertaken before decisions may be implemented.

VI. Environment

Enterprises play a key role in advancing sustainable economies and can contribute to delivering an effective and progressive response to global, regional and local environmental challenges, including the urgent threat of climate change. Within the framework of laws, regulations and administrative practices in the countries in which they operate, and in consideration of relevant international agreements, principles, objectives, and standards, enterprises should conduct their activities in a manner that takes due account of the need to protect the environment, and in turn workers, communities and society more broadly, avoids and addresses adverse environmental impacts and contributes to the wider goal of sustainable development. Enterprises can be involved in a range of adverse environmental impacts. These include, among others:

a) climate change;

b) biodiversity loss;

c) degradation of land, marine and freshwater ecosystems;

d) deforestation;

e) air, water and soil pollution;

f) mismanagement of waste, including hazardous substances

Important differences across environmental impacts are outlined in the commentary to this chapter, including with respect to climate change and how an individual enterprise's relationship to such impacts should be considered in the context of relevant frameworks.

In particular, enterprises should:

1. Establish and maintain a system of environmental management appropriate to the enterprise associated with the operations, products and services of the enterprise over their full life cycle, including by carrying out risk-based due diligence, as described in Chapter II, for adverse environmental impacts, including through:
    a) identifying and assessing adverse environmental impacts associated with an enterprise's operations, products or services, including through collection and evaluation of adequate and timely information regarding the adverse impacts associated with their operations, products and services and where activities may have significant adverse environmental impacts, preparing an appropriate environmental impact assessment;
    b) establishing and implementing measurable objectives, targets and strategies for addressing adverse environmental impacts associated with their operations, products and services and for improving environmental performance. Targets should be science-based, consistent with relevant national policies and international commitments, goals, and informed by best practice;
    c) regularly verifying the effectiveness of strategies and monitoring progress toward environmental objectives and targets, and periodically reviewing the continued relevance of objectives, targets and strategies;

   d) providing the public, workers, and other relevant stakeholders with adequate, measurable, verifiable (where applicable) and timely information on environmental impacts associated with their operations, products and services based on best available information, and progress against targets and objectives as described in paragraph 1.b;
   e) providing for, or co-operating in, remediation as necessary to address adverse environmental impacts the enterprise has caused or contributed to, and using leverage to influence other entities causing or contributing to adverse environmental impacts to remediate them.
2. Conduct meaningful engagement with relevant stakeholders affected by adverse environmental impacts associated with an enterprise's operations, products or services.
3. Consistent with the scientific and technical understanding of the risks, where there are threats of serious or irreversible damage to the environment, taking also into account human health and safety, not use the lack of full scientific certainty or pathways as a reason for postponing cost-effective measures to prevent or minimise such damage.
4. Maintain contingency plans for preventing, mitigating, and controlling serious environmental and health damage from their operations, including accidents and emergencies; and mechanisms for immediate reporting to the competent authorities.
5. Continually seek to improve environmental performance, at the level of the enterprise and, where appropriate, entities with which they have a business relationship, including by:
   a) adopting technologies, where feasible best available technologies, to improve environmental performance;
   b) developing and providing products or services that have no undue environmental impacts; are safe in their intended use; are durable, reparable and can be reused, recycled, or disposed of safely and that are produced in an environmentally sound manner that uses natural resources sustainably, minimises as far as possible energy and material input as well as generation of pollution, greenhouse gas emissions and waste, in particular hazardous waste;
   c) promoting higher levels of awareness among customers of the environmental implications of using the products and services of the enterprise, including by providing relevant and accurate information on their environmental impacts (for example, on greenhouse gas emissions, impacts on biodiversity, resource efficiency, reparability and recyclability or other environmental issues).
6. Provide adequate education and training to workers in environmental, health and safety matters, including on the management of hazardous and non-hazardous materials and waste as well as the prevention of environmental accidents, as well as more general environmental management areas, such as environmental impact assessment procedures, public relations, and environmental technologies. Providing support, including capacity building on environmental management, to suppliers and other business relationships, particularly small- and medium-sized enterprises and small holders, where appropriate and feasible.
7. Contribute to the development of environmentally responsible and economically efficient public policy, for example, by means of partnerships or initiatives that will enhance environmental awareness and protection.

Commentary on Chapter VI: Environment

66. Achieving environmental objectives requires a whole of society approach. The *Guidelines* set out expectations on how enterprises should avoid and address adverse environmental impacts and contribute to reaching the goals of climate change mitigation and adaptation; the conservation, restoration, and sustainable use of biological diversity; the sustainable, efficient and lawful use of land, resources and energy; sustainable consumption and production including through promotion of circular economy approaches; and pollution prevention, reduction and control. International commitments, multilateral agreements and other regulatory frameworks represent an important benchmark for understanding environmental issues and expectations. Some international agreements contain collective government objectives and may not provide detailed prescriptions regarding the responsibilities of individual enterprises in relation to such objectives. In such cases, relevant regulatory frameworks, national policy and widely recognised standards of environmental management and safeguards, and scientific evidence are important references. The text of the Environment Chapter broadly reflects the principles and objectives contained in the Rio Declaration on Environment and Development, in Agenda 21 (within the Rio Declaration) and the United Nations 2030 Agenda for Sustainable Development. It is also consistent with the UN Framework Convention on Climate Change (UNFCCC), the Paris Agreement, the Convention on Biological Diversity, Kunming-Montreal Global Biodiversity Framework, relevant regional conventions on access to information, public participation, and justice in environmental matters, the UN Convention to Combat Desertification, relevant regional environmental agreements, and reflects standards contained in such instruments as the ISO Standard on Environmental Management Systems, the International Finance Corporation's Environmental and Social Performance Standards, and Strategic Approach to International Chemicals Management (SAICM).

67. In the context of the *Guidelines*, "environmental management" should be interpreted in its broadest sense, embodying activities aimed at understanding environmental impacts and risks, avoiding and addressing environmental impacts related to an enterprise's operations, products and services, taking into consideration the enterprise's share of cumulative impacts and continually seeking to improve an enterprise's environmental performance. Environmental management also involves carrying out risk-based due diligence with respect to adverse environmental impacts. In line with Chapter II, the nature and extent of environmental due diligence will depend on the circumstances of a particular enterprise. Limitations to carrying out environmental due diligence may include lack of availability of environmental data or technologies. Due diligence will also involve risk-based prioritisation. It will also depend on the extent to which environmental impacts associated with the enterprise's operations, products or services are reasonably foreseeable. Environmental management is an important part of sustainable development and may involve reconciling a broad range of priorities, including those set out in national priorities and targets for sustainable development. Environmental management is both a business responsibility and a business opportunity. Multinational enterprises have a role to play in both respects. Managers of these enterprises should therefore give appropriate attention to environmental issues within their business strategies. Improving environmental performance requires a commitment to a systematic approach and to continual improvement of the system. An environmental management system provides the internal framework necessary to integrate environmental considerations into business operations. Having such a system in place should help to assure shareholders, workers, communities and other relevant stakeholders that the enterprise is actively working to protect the environment, from the adverse impact of its activities.

68. The chapeau of this chapter specifies a non-exhaustive list of adverse environmental impacts that may be associated with business activities. Many enterprise activities can entail adverse impacts on the environment. Adverse environmental impacts are significant changes in the environment or biota which have harmful effects on the composition, resilience, productivity or carrying capacity of natural and managed ecosystems, or on the operation of socio-economic systems or on people. Adverse environmental impacts should be assessed in light of best available science. Under the *Guidelines*, as

outlined in Chapter II, an enterprise "causes" an adverse environmental impact if its activities on their own are sufficient to result in the adverse impact. An enterprise "contributes to" an adverse environmental impact if its activities, in combination with the activities of other entities cause the impact, or if the activities of the enterprise cause, facilitate or incentivise another entity to cause an adverse impact. Adverse environmental impacts can also be directly linked to an enterprise's business operations, products or services by a business relationship, even if they do not contribute to those impacts.

69. Environmental impacts can be collective and interlinked, or isolated; they can be localised or transboundary in nature. While some environmental impacts are well understood, the extent, nature and cause of others may be less well understood, evolving, or even unknown. Therefore, while in some instances it will be possible to assess, based on available science and information, to what extent an enterprise is contributing to an adverse environmental impact, in other instances such an assessment may be challenging. In the context of the latter situation, for the purposes of the *Guidelines*, the assessment of an enterprise's contribution to adverse impacts should consider the extent to which its activities are consistent with widely recognised standards, environmental management processes and safeguards regarding good environmental practice; benchmarks and standards established in applicable environmental rules and regulatory frameworks; and relevant international agreements.

70. Adverse environmental impacts are often closely interlinked with other matters covered by the *Guidelines* such as health and safety, impacts to workers and communities, access to livelihoods or land tenure rights. Furthermore, carrying out environmental due diligence and managing adverse environmental impacts will often involve taking into account multiple environmental, social and developmental priorities. Notably the Paris Agreement preamble takes into account the imperatives of a just transition, of the workforce and the creation of decent work and quality jobs in accordance with nationally defined development priorities, and acknowledges that when taking action to address climate change, Parties should respect, promote and consider their respective obligations. In this respect it is important for enterprises to assess and address social impacts in the context of their environmental management and due diligence activities and to take action to prevent and mitigate such adverse impacts both in their transition away from environmentally harmful practices, as well as towards greener industries or practices, such as the use of renewable energy. Respecting labour rights, including engaging in social dialogue and collective bargaining, as outlined in Chapter V, meaningfully engaging with relevant stakeholders and, where relevant practicing responsible disengagement, as outlined in Chapter II, will be important in this respect.

71. In addition to improving environmental performance, instituting an environmental management system can provide economic benefits to enterprises through reduced operating and insurance costs, improved energy and resource conservation, reduced compliance and liability charges, increased sustainability and resilience, improved access to capital and skills, improved customer satisfaction, and improved community and public relations.

72. Communication regarding environmental impacts associated with an enterprise's operations, products and services, as well as meaningful stakeholder engagement, are a component of due diligence and may also be required by law. Reporting standards such as the Global Reporting Initiative and other environmental reporting standards provide useful references. See also Chapter III on Disclosure. Meaningful engagement and communication with stakeholders such as employees, customers, investors, suppliers, contractors, local communities, individuals or groups in situations of vulnerability or marginalisation, persons possessing special rights or legitimate tenure rights, and Indigenous Peoples, and with the public-at-large is particularly important where they are or may be affected by such impacts and where scarce or at-risk environmental assets are at stake, either in a regional, national or international context.

73. Enterprises are encouraged to adopt sustainable consumption and production patterns, including, through resource efficiency, the circular economy and other models. Through such practices enterprises

can significantly reduce their adverse environmental impacts. Resource efficiency promotes more efficient and effective use of resources and materials, including through environmentally sound raw material supply. Further, circular economy approaches are relevant, as appropriate, as one of the means available to achieve sustainable development. According to national priorities and circumstances, a circular economy is a model in which products and materials are designed so that they can be reused, repaired, remanufactured, recycled or recovered and therefore maintained in the economy for as long as possible, along with the resources they are made of, and in which the generation of waste, especially hazardous waste, is avoided or minimised, and greenhouse gas emissions are prevented and reduced.

74. The basic premise of the *Guidelines* is that enterprises should act as soon as possible, and in a proactive way, to avoid adverse environmental impacts.

75. The *Guidelines* are not intended to reinterpret any existing instruments or to create new commitments or precedents on the part of governments – they are intended only to recommend how the precautionary approach should be implemented at the level of enterprises. It is recognised that some flexibility is needed in the application of this approach, based on the specific context in which it is carried out. It is also recognised that governments determine the basic framework in this field in light of their capabilities and have the responsibility to consult periodically with stakeholders on the most appropriate ways forward, ensuring transparency and a science-based approach.

76. Enterprises have an important role in contributing towards net- zero greenhouse gas emissions and a climate-resilient economy, necessary for achieving internationally agreed goals on climate change mitigation and adaptation. During the process of transitioning to net-zero greenhouse gas emissions, many business activities will involve some level of emissions of greenhouse gases or reduction of carbon sinks. Enterprises should ensure that their greenhouse gas emissions and impact on carbon sinks are consistent with internationally agreed global temperature goals based on best available science, including as assessed by the Intergovernmental Panel on Climate Change (IPCC).

77. This includes the introduction and implementation of science-based policies, strategies and transition plans on climate change mitigation and adaptation as well as adopting, implementing, monitoring and reporting on short, medium and long-term mitigation targets. These targets should be science-based, include absolute and also, where relevant, intensity-based GHG reduction targets and take into account scope 1, 2, and, to the extent possible based on best available information, scope 3 GHG emissions. It will be important to report against, review and update targets regularly in relation to their adequacy and relevance, based on the latest available scientific evidence and as different national or industry specific transition pathways are developed and updated. Enterprises should prioritise eliminating or reducing sources of emissions over offsetting, compensation, or neutralization measures. Carbon credits, or offsets may be considered as a means to address unabated emissions as a last resort. Carbon credits or offsets should be of high environmental integrity and should not draw attention away from the need to reduce emissions and should not contribute to locking-in greenhouse gas intensive processes and infrastructures. Enterprises should report publicly on their reliance on, and relevant characteristics of, any carbon credits or offsets. Such reporting should be distinct from and complementary to reporting on emissions reduction.

78. The use of leverage and provision of technology on mutually acceptable terms, technical assistance and funding to suppliers and other business relationships for climate mitigation and adaptation efforts will be crucial for meeting targets and addressing impacts.

79. Achieving climate resilience and adaptation is a critical component of the long-term global response to climate change to protect people and ecosystems and will require the engagement and support of all segments of society. Enterprises should avoid activities, which undermine climate adaptation for, and resilience of, communities, workers and ecosystems.

80. The conservation of biological diversity and sustainable management and use of natural resources and ecosystems, including, for example, forests, oceans, peatlands and wetlands, is highly important to

human health and livelihoods, species survival as well as mitigation of and adaptation to climate change. Enterprises should contribute to the conservation of biological diversity, the sustainable use of their components, and the fair and equitable sharing of the benefits arising out of the utilisation of genetic resources. Enterprises should also avoid and address land, marine and freshwater degradation, including deforestation, in line with objectives of UN Sustainable Development Goals, notably 15.2, the UN Strategic Plan for Forests 2017–2030 and the 2021 Glasgow Leaders' Declaration on Forests and Land Use which seek to halt and reverse forest loss and land degradation by 2030. Efforts should include carrying out heightened due diligence with respect to potential adverse impacts on biodiversity in national parks, reserves and other protected areas, including UNESCO Natural World Heritage sites, areas protected in fulfilment of the Convention on Biological Diversity, and as defined in domestic law, as well as on protected species. Where appropriate, and according to their own capacities and domestic laws where they operate, enterprises should also contribute to sustainable land and forest management, including restoration, afforestation, reforestation including reduction of land, marine and freshwater degradation. Enterprises' efforts to prevent or mitigate adverse impacts on biodiversity should be guided by the biodiversity mitigation hierarchy, which recommends first seeking to avoid damage to biodiversity, reducing or minimising it where avoidance is not possible, and using offsets and restoration as a last resort for adverse impacts that cannot be avoided.

81. Adverse environmental impacts, particularly in the context of biodiversity and land, marine and freshwater degradation, can be related to the responsible governance of tenure of land, forests, and fisheries. As noted in the Voluntary Guidelines on the Responsible Governance of Tenure, of Land, Fisheries and Forests in the Context of National Food Security (VGGTs), the responsible governance of tenure of lands, forests and fisheries can play a role in supporting sustainable use of the environment. In this context, the VGGTs call for investments that do no harm, and safeguard against dispossession of legitimate tenure right holders and environmental damage.

82. The *Guidelines* also encourage enterprises to work to raise the level of environmental performance in all parts of their operations, even where this may not be formally required by existing practice in the countries in which they operate. In this regard, enterprises should take due account of their social and economic effects on developing countries.

83. For example, multinational enterprises often have access to existing and innovative technologies or operating procedures which could, if applied, help raise environmental performance overall. Multinational enterprises are frequently regarded as leaders in their respective fields, so the potential for a "demonstration effect" on other enterprises should not be overlooked. Ensuring that the environment of the countries in which multinational enterprises operate also benefit from available and innovative technologies and practices is an important way of building support for international investment activities more generally.

84. Enterprises have an important role to play in the training and education of their employees and other stakeholders with regard to environmental management matters. They are encouraged to discharge this responsibility in as broad a manner as possible, especially in areas directly related to human health and safety. Enterprises should also communicate their environmental policies, requirements and standards in a clear and accessible way to their business relationships.

85. Enterprises should respect animal welfare standards that are aligned with the World Organisation for Animal Health (WOAH) Terrestrial Code. An animal experiences good welfare if the animal is healthy, comfortable, well nourished, safe, is not suffering from unpleasant states such as pain, fear and distress, and is able to express behaviours that are important for its physical and mental state. Good animal welfare requires disease prevention and appropriate veterinary care, shelter, management and nutrition, a stimulating and safe environment, humane handling and humane slaughter or killing. In addition, enterprises should adhere to guidance for the transport of live animals developed by relevant international organisations.

VII. Combating Bribery and Other Forms of Corruption

Adverse impacts on matters covered by the *Guidelines* are often enabled by means of corruption. As such, an enterprise's implementation of effective anticorruption measures is an important contribution to the avoidance of other adverse impacts covered by the *Guidelines*. Enterprises should not engage in any act of bribery or other forms of corruption.

In particular, enterprises should:

1. Not engage in any act of corruption, including the offering, promising or giving of any undue pecuniary or other advantage to public officials or employees of persons or entities with which an enterprise has a business relationship or to their relatives or associates. Likewise, enterprises should not request, agree to or accept any undue pecuniary or other advantage from public officials or the employees of persons or entities with which an enterprise has a business relationship. Enterprises should not use third parties or other intermediaries, including, *inter alia*, agents, consultants, representatives, distributors, consortia, contractors and suppliers and joint venture partners for channelling undue pecuniary or other advantages to public officials, or to employees of persons or entities with which an enterprise has a business relationship or to their relatives or associates.
2. Develop and adopt adequate internal controls, ethics and compliance programmes or measures for adequately preventing, detecting and addressing bribery and other forms of corruption, developed on the basis of a risk-based assessment, taking in to account the individual circumstances of an enterprise, in particular the enterprise risk factors related to bribery and other forms of corruption (including, *inter alia*, its geographical and industrial sector of operation, other responsible business conduct issues, the regulatory environment, the type of business relationships, transactions with foreign governments, and use of third parties). These internal controls, ethics and compliance programmes or measures should include a system of financial and accounting procedures, including a system of internal controls, reasonably designed to ensure the maintenance of fair and accurate books, conflict of interest registers, records, and accounts, to ensure that they cannot be used for the purpose of engaging in or hiding bribery or other acts of corruption. Such individual circumstances and risks should be regularly monitored and re-assessed as necessary to determine the allocation of compliance resources and to ensure the enterprise's internal controls, ethics and compliance programme or measures are adapted and continue to be effective, and to mitigate the risk of enterprises becoming involved in bribery or other forms of corruption. These internal controls, ethics and compliance programmes or measures for preventing and detecting all forms of corruption should also include carrying out risk-based due diligence as described in Chapter II.
3. Prohibit or discourage, in internal company controls, ethics and compliance programmes or measures, the use of small facilitation payments, which are generally illegal in the countries where they are made, and, when such payments are made, accurately record these in books and financial records.

4. Ensure, taking into account the particular risks related to bribery and other forms of corruption, properly documented due diligence pertaining to the hiring, as well as the appropriate and regular oversight of agents, and that remuneration of agents is appropriate and for legitimate services only. Where relevant, an updated list of agents engaged in connection with transactions with public bodies and State-owned enterprises should be kept and made available to competent authorities, in accordance with applicable public disclosure requirements. Enterprises should take steps to ensure that their agents avoid exercising illicit influence and comply with professional standards in their relations with public officials.
5. Enhance the transparency of their activities in the fight against bribery and other forms of corruption and foster a culture of integrity. Measures could include *i)* strong, explicit and visible support and commitment from the board of directors or equivalent governing body and senior management to the enterprise's internal controls, ethics and compliance programmes; *ii)* a clearly articulated and visible corporate policy prohibiting bribery and other forms of corruption, easily accessible to all employees and relevant third parties, including, *inter alia*, foreign subsidiaries, agents, and other intermediaries; and *iii)* disclosing the management systems and the internal controls, ethics and compliance programmes or measures adopted by enterprises in order to honour these commitments. Enterprises should also foster openness and dialogue with the public so as to promote its awareness of and co-operation in the fight against bribery other forms of corruption. Enterprises are encouraged to disclose, without prejudice to national laws and requirements, any misconduct related to bribery and other forms of corruption, as well as the measures adopted to address cases of suspected bribery and other forms of corruption. These measures may include, but are not limited to, processes for identifying, investigating, and reporting the misconduct and genuinely and proactively engaging with law enforcement authorities.
6. Promote awareness of and compliance with enterprise policies and internal controls, ethics and compliance programmes or measures against bribery and other forms of corruption, among employees and persons or entities linked by a business relationship, through appropriate dissemination of such policies, programmes or measures and through training programmes and disciplinary procedures that take into account applicable language, cultural and technological barriers.
7. Not make illegal contributions to candidates for public office or to political parties or to other organisations linked to political parties or political candidates. Political contributions should fully comply with national laws including public disclosure requirements and should require senior management approval. This includes not obliging workers to support a political candidate or a political organisation.

Commentary on Chapter VII: Combating Bribery and Other Forms of Corruption

86. The terms bribery and other forms of corruption should be interpreted consistently with the below instruments. Corruption includes the bribery of public officials or the employees of persons or entities linked by business relationships. It may also encompass trading in influence, embezzlement and misuse of sponsorships and charitable donations. Enterprises should not, for example, directly or indirectly, offer, promise, give, or demand a bribe or other undue advantage to obtain or retain business or other improper advantage. Enterprises should also resist the solicitation of bribes and extortion. While a conflict of interest is not ipso facto corruption, there is increasing recognition that conflicts between the private interests and public duties of public officials, if inadequately managed, could potentially result in corruption. The *Convention on Combating Bribery of Foreign Public Officials in International Business Transactions [OECD/LEGAL/0293]* (the *OECD Anti-Bribery Convention*) entered into force on 15 February 1999. The *OECD Anti-Bribery Convention*, along with the *Recommendation for Further Combating Bribery of Foreign Public Officials in International Business Transactions [OECD/LEGAL/0378]* (the *Anti-Bribery Recommendation*), *the*

Recommendation on Tax Measures for Further Combating Bribery of Foreign Public Officials in International Business Transactions [OECD/LEGAL/0371], the *Recommendation on Bribery and Officially Supported Export Credits* [OECD/LEGAL/0447] *and* the *Recommendation for Development Co-operation Actors on Managing the Risk of Corruption* [OECD/LEGAL/0431], are the core OECD instruments that address the offering side of the foreign bribery transaction. Collectively these instruments aim to eliminate the "supply" of bribes to foreign public officials, with each country taking responsibility for the activities of its enterprises and what happens within its own jurisdiction.[2] A programme of rigorous and systematic monitoring of countries' implementation of the *OECD Anti-Bribery Convention* and these related instruments has been established to promote their full implementation. Other acts of corruption and integrity risks are also addressed in the *Recommendation on Public Integrity* [OECD/LEGAL/0435]; the *Recommendation on Principles for Transparency and Integrity in Lobbying* [OECD/LEGAL/0379]; the *Recommendation on OECD Guidelines for Managing Conflict of Interest in the Public Service* [OECD/LEGAL/0316] and the *Recommendation on Guidelines on Anti-Corruption and Integrity in State-Owned Enterprises* [OECD/LEGAL/0451].

87. Corruption is damaging to democratic institutions and the governance of corporations. It discourages investment and distorts international competitive conditions. Beyond the economic impact, corruption can have harmful effects, including, *inter alia*, undermining global stability, lack of enforcement of environmental standards and labour rights, or provision of sub-standard goods. In particular, the diversion of funds through corrupt practices undermines attempts by citizens to achieve higher levels of economic, social and environmental welfare. Corruption disproportionately affects those belonging to marginalised or vulnerable groups or populations and can exacerbate gender inequalities. Enterprises have an important role to play in combating these practices by taking into account overlapping forms of structural discrimination related to ethnicity, race, sex, and sexual orientation, among other factors, when setting up controls, ethics and compliance programmes.

88. Propriety, integrity and transparency in both the public and private domains are key concepts in the fight against bribery and other forms of corruption. The business community, non-governmental organisations, governments and inter-governmental organisations should all co-operate to strengthen public support for anticorruption measures and to enhance transparency and public awareness of the problems of corruption and bribery. The adoption of appropriate corporate governance practices is also an essential element in fostering a culture of ethics within enterprises.

89. The *Anti-Bribery Recommendation* recommends in particular that governments encourage their enterprises to develop and adopt adequate internal controls, ethics and compliance programmes or measures for the purpose of preventing and detecting foreign bribery, taking into account the *Good Practice Guidance on Internal Controls, Ethics and Compliance*, included as Annex II to the *Anti-Bribery Recommendation*. This *Good Practice Guidance* is addressed to enterprises, including state-owned

---

[2] In the *OECD Anti-Bribery Convention*, the offence of foreign bribery is defined as the "...offer[ing], promis[ing], or giv[ing] of any undue pecuniary or other advantage, whether directly or through intermediaries, to a foreign public official, for that official or for a third party, in order that the official act or refrain from acting in relation to the performance of official duties, in order to obtain or retain business or other improper advantage in the conduct of international business". The Commentaries to the *OECD Anti-Bribery Convention* (paragraph 9) clarify that "small 'facilitation' payments do not constitute payments made 'to obtain or retain business or other improper advantage' within the meaning of paragraph 1 and, accordingly, are also not an offence. Such payments, which, in some countries, are made to induce public officials to perform their functions, such as issuing licenses or permits, are generally illegal in the foreign country concerned. Other countries can and should address this corrosive phenomenon by such means as support for programmes of good governance. The *Anti-Bribery Recommendation* (Section XIV.i) recommends that governments "undertake to periodically review their policies and approach on small facilitation payments in order to effectively combat the phenomenon".

enterprises, as well as business organisations and professional associations, and highlights good practices for ensuring the effectiveness of their internal controls, ethics and compliance programmes or measures to prevent and detect foreign bribery, including protections for reporting persons. It is flexible, and is intended to be adapted by enterprises, in particular small- and medium-sized enterprises, according to their individual circumstances, including their size, type, legal structure, and geographical and industrial sector of operation, as well as the jurisdictional and other basic legal principles under which they operate. In addition, for the purposes of these *Guidelines,* internal controls, ethics and compliance programmes or measures related to corruption should also include carrying out risk-based due diligence in line with the recommendations articulated in Chapter II.

90. Collective action and meaningful engagement with local and international civil society organisations, business, professional associations, and international organisations also may help enterprises to better design and implement effective enterprise anti-corruption policies and mitigate corruption risks one enterprise cannot mitigate individually.

91. The United Nations Convention against Corruption (UNCAC), which entered into force on 14 December 2005, sets out a broad range of standards, measures and rules to fight corruption. Under the UNCAC, States Parties are required to prohibit their officials from receiving bribes and their enterprises from bribing domestic public officials, as well as foreign public officials and officials of public international organisations, and to consider disallowing private to private bribery. The UNCAC and the *OECD Anti-Bribery Convention* are mutually supporting and complementary.

92. To address the demand side of bribery, good governance practices are important elements to prevent enterprises from being solicited to pay bribes. Both home and host governments should assist enterprises confronted with solicitation of bribes or other forms of corruption, raise awareness and provide training to relevant public officials, consider fostering collective action initiatives with private and public sector representatives, as well as civil society organisations and, where appropriate, undertake coordinated actions to address the solicitation and acceptance of bribes. The *Good Practice Guidance on Specific Articles of the Convention* in Annex II of the *Anti-Bribery Recommendation* states that the *OECD Anti-Bribery Convention* should be implemented in such a way that it does not provide a defence or exception where the foreign public official solicits a bribe. Furthermore, the UNCAC requires the criminalisation of bribe solicitation by domestic public officials.

VIII. Consumer Interests

When dealing with consumers, enterprises should act in accordance with fair business, marketing and advertising practices and should take all reasonable steps to ensure the quality and reliability of the goods and services that they provide. In particular, they should:

1. Ensure that the goods and services they provide meet all agreed or legally required standards for consumer health and safety, including those pertaining to health warnings and safety information, and do not pose an unreasonable risk to the health or safety of consumers in foreseeable use or foreseeable improper use or misuse.
2. Provide accurate, verifiable and clear information that is sufficient to enable consumers to make informed decisions, including information on the prices and, where appropriate, content, safe use, environmental attributes, maintenance, storage, disposal of goods and services, and relevant e-commerce disclosures such as privacy issues, and information about available dispute resolution and redress options. The information should be presented in a comprehensible and easily accessible manner using plain language, while also regarding the needs of accessibility for consumers with disabilities. Where feasible this information should be provided in a manner that facilitates consumers' ability to compare products.
3. Provide consumers with access to fair, easy to use, timely and effective non-judicial dispute resolution and redress mechanisms, without unnecessary cost or burden.
4. Not make representations or omissions, nor engage in any other practices that are deceptive, misleading, fraudulent unfair or that otherwise subvert consumer choice in ways that harm consumers or competition.
5. Support efforts to promote consumer education in areas that relate to their business activities, with the aim of, *inter alia*, improving the ability of consumers to: *i)* make informed decisions involving complex goods, services and markets, *ii)* better understand the economic, environmental and social impact of their decisions and *iii)* support sustainable consumption.
6. Protect consumer privacy by ensuring that enterprise practices relating to the collection and use of consumer data are lawful, transparent and fair, enable consumer participation and choice and take all reasonable measures to ensure the security of personal data that they collect, store, process or disseminate.
7. Co-operate fully with public authorities to prevent and combat abusive or deceptive marketing practices (including misleading advertising, and commercial fraud) and to diminish or prevent serious threats to public health and safety or to the environment deriving from the consumption, use or disposal of their goods and services.
8. Take into consideration, in applying the above principles, *i)* the needs of consumers, especially those who may be experiencing vulnerability or disadvantage, and *ii)* the specific challenges that e-commerce may pose for consumers.

Commentary on Chapter VIII: Consumer Interests

93. The chapter on consumer interests of the *Guidelines* draws on the work of the OECD Committee on Consumer Policy and the Committee on Financial Markets, relevant OECD standards in the area of consumer protection, as well as the work of other organisations, including the International Chamber of Commerce, the International Organization for Standardization and the United Nations, including the UN Environment Programme (i.e., the UN Guidelines on Consumer Policy) and relevant instruments, including the Advertising and Marketing Communications Code for global advertising and responsible marketing, International Chamber of Commerce.

94. The chapter recognises that consumer satisfaction and related interests constitute a fundamental basis for the successful operation of enterprises. It also recognises that consumer markets for goods and services have undergone major transformation over time. Regulatory reform, more open global markets, the development of new technologies which have transformed digital and financial services and the growth in consumer services have been key agents of change, providing consumers with greater choice and the other benefits which derive from more open competition. At the same time, the pace of change and increased complexity of many markets have generally made it more difficult for consumers to compare and assess goods and services. Moreover, consumer demographics have also changed over time. Children are becoming increasingly significant forces in the market, as are the growing number of older adults. While consumers are better educated overall, many still lack the arithmetic and literacy skills that are required in today's more complex, information-intensive marketplace. Further, many consumers are increasingly interested in knowing the position and activities of enterprises on a broad range of economic, social and environmental issues, and in taking these into account when choosing goods and services.

95. The chapeau calls on enterprises to apply fair business, marketing and advertising practices and to ensure the quality and reliability of the products that they provide. These principles, it is noted, apply to both goods and services.

96. Paragraph 1 underscores the importance for enterprises to adhere to required health and safety standards and the importance for them to provide consumers with adequate health and safety information on their products.

97. Paragraph 2 concerns information disclosure. It calls for enterprises to provide information which is sufficient for consumers to make informed decisions. The way information is provided in the online area should be tailored and adapted to the consumer's means of access. This would include information on the financial risks associated with products, where relevant. Furthermore, in some instances enterprises are legally required to provide information in a manner that enables consumers to make direct comparisons of goods and services (for example, unit pricing). In the absence of direct legislation, enterprises are encouraged to present information, when dealing with consumers, in a way that facilitates comparisons of goods and services and enables consumers to easily determine what the total cost of a product will be. It should be noted that what is considered to be "sufficient" can change over time and enterprises should be responsive to these changes. Any product and environmental or social claims that enterprises make should be based on adequate evidence and, as applicable, proper tests and verification. Claims may apply both to the way a product or service was produced and to the attributes of the product or service itself. Given consumers' growing interest in environmental and social issues and sustainable consumption, information should be provided, as appropriate, on the environmental or social attributes of products and services. This could include information on the energy efficiency and the degree of recyclability, durability, and reparability of products, the sustainability attributes of financial products and services or, for example, in the case of food products, information on agricultural practices or nutritional attributes.

98. Business conduct is increasingly considered by consumers when making their purchasing decisions. Enterprises are therefore encouraged to make information available on initiatives they have taken to integrate social and environmental concerns into their business operations and to otherwise

support sustainable consumption. Chapter III of the *Guidelines* on Disclosure is relevant in this regard. Enterprises are therefore encouraged to communicate value statements or statements of business conduct to the public, including information on the social, ethical and environmental policies of the enterprise and other codes of conduct to which the enterprise subscribes. Enterprises are encouraged to make this information available in plain language and ensure the accuracy of any claim regarding environmental or social performance. Growth in the number of enterprises reporting in these areas and targeting information to consumers would be welcome.

99. Paragraph 3 reflects language that is used in the *Recommendation on Consumer Dispute Resolution and Redress [OECD/LEGAL/0356]*. The Recommendation establishes a framework for developing effective approaches to address consumer complaints, including a series of actions that industry can take in this respect. It is noted that the mechanisms that many enterprises have established to resolve consumer disputes have helped increase consumer confidence and consumer satisfaction. These mechanisms can provide more practicable solutions to complaints than legal actions, which can be expensive, difficult and time consuming for all the parties involved. For these non-judicial mechanisms to be effective, however, consumers need to be made aware of their existence and would benefit from guidance on how to file complaints, especially when claims involve cross-border or multi- dimensional transactions.

100. Paragraph 4 concerns deceptive, misleading, fraudulent and other unfair commercial practices. Such practices can distort markets, at the expense of both consumers and responsible enterprises and should be avoided.

101. Paragraph 5 concerns consumer education, which has taken on greater importance with the growing complexity of many markets and products. Governments, consumer organisations and many enterprises have recognised that this is a shared responsibility and that they can play important roles in this regard. The difficulties that consumers have experienced in evaluating complex products in financial and other areas have underscored the importance for stakeholders to work together to promote education aimed at improving consumer decision-making.

102. Paragraph 6 concerns personal data. The increasing collection and use of personal data by enterprises can pose great risks to the privacy of consumers and their well-being. The protection of personal data of consumers, including data security, is therefore of great importance.

103. Paragraph 7 underscores the importance of enterprises to work with public authorities to help prevent and combat deceptive marketing practices more effectively. Co-operation is also called for to diminish or prevent risks to public health and safety and to the environment. This includes risks associated with the disposal of goods, as well as their consumption and use. This reflects recognition of the importance of considering and managing risks to the safety of products throughout their lifetime, in particular at the design, manufacture, distribution, use and disposal stages.

104. Paragraph 8 calls on enterprises to take the situations of vulnerable and disadvantaged consumers into account when they market goods and services. Disadvantaged or vulnerable consumers refer to particular consumers or categories of consumers, who because of personal characteristics or circumstances (like age, mental or physical capacity, education, income, language or remote location) may meet particular difficulties in operating in today's information-intensive, globalised markets. The paragraph also highlights the growing importance of mobile and other forms of e-commerce in global markets. The benefits that such commerce provides are significant and growing. But there are also risks for consumer harm. Governments have spent considerable time examining ways to ensure that consumers are afforded transparent and effective protection that is not less in the case of e- commerce than the level of protection afforded in more traditional forms of commerce. It is therefore important that enterprises take steps to reduce the risks of e-commerce so that the level of protection is not less than that provided in more traditional forms of commerce.

IX. Science, Technology and Innovation

Scientific research and technological innovation have driven productivity in all sectors, as well as the ability of enterprises to conduct due diligence and contribute to sustainable development. Enterprises should, as appropriate, contribute to the development of local and national innovative capacity. In the context of development, financing, sale, licensing, trade and use of technology, including gathering and using data, as well as scientific research and innovation, enterprises should observe the *Guidelines* and comply with applicable national laws and requirements, including privacy and data protection requirements and export control regulations. In particular, enterprises should:

1. Carry out risk-based due diligence, as described in Chapter II, with respect to actual and potential adverse impacts related to science, technology and innovation.
2. Adopt, where practicable in the course of their business activities, practices that enable the voluntary, safe, secure and efficient transfer of technology and know-how on mutually agreed terms, as well as enhance access to and sharing of data to foster scientific discovery and innovations with due regard to the protection of intellectual property rights, confidentiality obligations, privacy, personal data protection, export controls and non-discrimination principles.
3. When appropriate, perform science and technology development activities in host countries to address local market needs, as well as employ host country personnel in science and technology development activities, and encourage and support their training, taking into account integrity, security and commercial needs.
4. When granting licenses for the use of intellectual property rights or when otherwise voluntarily transferring technology, do so on mutually agreed terms and conditions, with appropriate safeguards to prevent and mitigate adverse impacts, and in a manner that contributes to the longterm sustainable development prospects of the host country and respects export control regulations.
5. Where relevant to commercial objectives, develop ties with local higher education institutions, public research institutions and participate in co-operative research projects with local industry or industry associations, including small- and medium-sized enterprises and civil society organisations. Such co-operation should take into account effective risk management, ethical considerations, national security concerns, applicable laws and considerations of stakeholders. It should also recognise the value of open science and respect safeguards to preserve academic freedom, as well as research and scientific autonomy.
6. When collecting, sharing and using data, enhance transparency of data access and sharing arrangements, and encourage the adoption, throughout the data value cycle, of responsible data governance practices that meet standards and obligations that are applicable, widely recognised or accepted among Adherents to the *Guidelines*, including codes of conduct, ethical principles, rules regarding manipulation and coercion of consumers, and privacy and data protection norms.
7. Enterprises should support, as appropriate to their circumstances, co-operative efforts in the appropriate fora to promote an open, free, global, interoperable, reliable, accessible, affordable, secure and resilient Internet, including through respect of the freedoms of expression, peaceful assembly and association online, and consistent with the matters covered by the *Guidelines*.

Commentary on Chapter IX: Science, Technology and Innovation

105. The development, licensing, sale, trade and use of technology has a profound impact on the matters covered by the Guidelines, including sustainable development, human rights, economic participation, the quality of democracy, social cohesion, climate change, the global business and labour landscape and market dynamics. Scientific research and technological innovation has driven productivity in all sectors, as well as the ability of enterprises to conduct due diligence and contribute to sustainable development, but can also be associated with challenges and adverse impacts.

106. Given the evolving nature of this topic and the fact that it touches on many issues, the scope of this chapter is meant to be broad and inclusive to ensure its continued relevance in relation to risks associated with future science, technology and innovation developments.

107. In a knowledge-based and globalised economy the ability to access and utilise technology, data and know-how is essential for improving enterprise performance. Such access is also important for the realisation of the economy-wide effects of technological progress, including productivity growth and job creation, within the context of sustainable development.[3] Multinational enterprises are an important conduit of technology transfer across borders. They can contribute to the national innovative capacity of their host countries by generating, diffusing, and even enabling the use of new technologies by domestic enterprises and institutions. The research and development activities of multinational enterprises and investments in new technologies, when well connected to the national innovation system, can help enhance the economic and social progress in their host countries. In turn, the development of a dynamic innovation system in the host country expands commercial opportunities for multinational enterprises.

108. The chapter thus aims to promote the diffusion, by multinational enterprises, of the fruits of research and development activities among the countries where they operate, contributing thereby to the innovative capacities of host countries, within the limits imposed by economic feasibility, competitiveness concerns, and in line with privacy, data protection, security, intellectual property protection and confidentiality obligations. In this regard, fostering technology diffusion may include the commercialisation of products and services which imbed new technology, licensing of process innovations, hiring and training of science and technology personnel and development of research and development co-operative ventures. When selling or licensing technology, not only should the terms and conditions negotiated be mutually agreed, but multinational enterprises should consider the long-term developmental, environmental and societal impacts of technology. In their activities, multinational enterprises can establish and improve the innovative capacity of their international subsidiaries, subcontractors, and other entities with which they have business relationships. In addition, multinational enterprises can call attention to the importance of local scientific and technological infrastructure, both physical and institutional. In this regard, multinational enterprises can usefully contribute to the formulation by host country governments of policy frameworks conducive to the development of dynamic innovation systems.

109. Science is understood here as including, among other issues, research and exploration. Technology is understood here to include digital technology, non-digital technology, and digital services, as well as digital ecosystems that facilitate their development and use. Innovation is understood here as the process of developing a new or improved product, service or process with the intent of making it available to potential users or bringing it into use by the enterprise.

110. Data is understood here, as in relevant OECD Recommendations, to refer to recorded information in structured or unstructured formats, including text, images, sound, and video. Data-driven innovation and

---

[3] Paragraph 7 is without prejudice to positions held by governments in the area of electronic commerce at the World Trade Organisation (WTO). It is not intended to disregard other important public policy interests which may relate to the use of the internet which would need to be taken into account. Some countries have referred to the 2005 Tunis Agenda for the Information Society in this regard.

data-intensive science hold immense promise to address grand societal challenges. Open science initiatives and access to data have had far-reaching effects on the reproducibility of scientific results, diffusion of knowledge across society, cross-disciplinary co-operation, resource efficiency, productivity and competitiveness. Data flows across borders are critical to support international commerce, information and knowledge exchange to bridge digital divides and sustainable development. Paragraph 2 reinforces these benefits, but also acknowledges risks of the theft, as well as irresponsible sharing and use of data that may undermine individual privacy and may pose potential national security risks. Enterprises in the data ecosystem, including data holders, data producers, and data intermediaries, as defined in the *Recommendation on Enhancing Access to and Sharing of Data [OECD/LEGAL/0463],* are encouraged to consider recommendations on responsible data access, sharing and use as outlined in the said Recommendation, which seeks to ensure implementation of risk management measures throughout the data value cycle, including measures necessary to protect the confidentiality, integrity, security and availability of data, particularly in the context of managing biological data such as DNA, and when disclosing data to law enforcement and other government agencies.

111. In paragraph 4, the expectations on enterprises are meant to be proportional to avoid terms and conditions, which result in unintended consequences. Enterprises should also make efforts to identify situations where certain actors may seek to benefit from technology transfer in order to misuse civilian technology.

112. In line with Chapter II, the nature and extent of due diligence for adverse impacts related to science, technology and innovation will depend on the circumstances of a particular situation and will involve risk-based prioritisation. This should also take into account known or reasonably foreseeable circumstances related to the use of the product or service provided in accordance with its intended purpose, or under conditions of reasonably foreseeable improper use or misuse, which may give rise to adverse impacts.

113. Enterprises involved in the development of new technology or new applications of existing tools should anticipate to the extent feasible and, as appropriate, address ethical, legal, labour, social and environmental challenges raised by novel technology while promoting responsible innovation and engaging in dialogue and information sharing with local regulatory authorities and worker representatives. In addition to and as supported in the implementation of the recommendations of the Guidelines, enterprises are encouraged to consider available guidance on the innovation process, including relevant OECD standards in the area of artificial intelligence and neurotechnology, including the *Recommendation on Artificial Intelligence* [OECD/LEGAL/0449] and the *Recommendation on Responsible Innovation in Neurotechnology [OECD/LEGAL/0457]*.

114. Digital security is a shared responsibility across all stakeholders, including businesses, customers and governments. Digital security incidents, such as unauthorised access to systems or software, compromised accounts, loss or theft of data, or interference with IT resources, can harm businesses, governments and individuals by undermining the availability, integrity and/or confidentiality of their data, information systems and networks. Enterprises should conduct digital security risk management in a manner that is consistent with the other chapters of the Guidelines. Privacy-by-design principles, use of strong encryption, permission and access management protocols, and other best practices can reduce threats and mitigate harm. Enterprises should also take into account relevant OECD standards in the area of data.

115. In all activities concerning children and youth participation in, or engagement with the digital environment, enterprises should take into account, as appropriate, the child's best interests as a primary consideration and in their due diligence identify how the rights of children and youth can be respected and the well-being of children and youth can be protected and promoted in the digital environment, and take appropriate measures to do so consistent with the *Recommendation on Children in the Digital Environment [OECD/LEGAL/0389]* and the OECD *Guidelines for Digital Service Providers*.

X. Competition

Enterprises should:

1. Carry out their activities in a manner consistent with all applicable competition laws and regulations, taking into account the competition laws of all jurisdictions in which the activities may have anti- competitive effects.

2. Refrain from entering into or carrying out anti-competitive agreements among competitors, including agreements to:

   a) fix prices;

   b) make rigged bids (collusive tenders);

   c) establish output restrictions or quotas; or

   d) share or divide markets by allocating customers, suppliers, territories or lines of commerce.

3. Co-operate with investigating competition authorities by, among other things and subject to applicable law and appropriate safeguards, providing responses as promptly and completely as practicable to requests for information, and considering the use of available instruments, such as waivers of confidentiality where appropriate, to promote effective and efficient co-operation among investigating authorities.

4. Regularly promote employee awareness of the importance of compliance with all applicable competition laws and regulations, and, in particular, train senior management of the enterprise in relation to competition issues.

Commentary on Chapter X: Competition

116. These recommendations emphasise the importance of competition laws and regulations to the efficient operation of both domestic and international markets and reaffirm the importance of compliance with those laws and regulations by domestic and multinational enterprises. They also seek to ensure that all enterprises are aware of developments concerning the scope, remedies and sanctions of competition laws and the extent of co-operation among competition authorities. The term "competition" law is used to refer to laws, including both "antitrust" and "antimonopoly" laws, that variously prohibit: a) anti-competitive agreements; b) the abuse of market power or of dominance; c) the acquisition of market power or dominance by means other than efficient performance; or d) the substantial lessening of competition or the significant impeding of effective competition through mergers or acquisitions.

117. In general, competition laws and policies prohibit: a) hard core cartels; b) other anti-competitive agreements; c) anti-competitive conduct that exploits or extends market dominance or market power; and d) anti- competitive mergers and acquisitions. Under the *Recommendation Concerning Effective Action Against Hard Core Cartels* [OECD/LEGAL/0452], the anticompetitive agreements referred to in sub a) constitute hard core cartels, but the Recommendation incorporates differences in member countries' laws, including differences in the laws' exemptions or provisions allowing for an exception or authorisation for activity that might otherwise be prohibited. The recommendations in these *Guidelines* do not suggest that

enterprises should forego availing themselves of such legally available exemptions or provisions. The categories sub b) and c) are more general because the effects of other kinds of agreements and of unilateral conduct are more ambiguous, and there is less consensus on what should be considered anti-competitive.

118. The goal of competition policy is to contribute to overall welfare and economic growth by promoting market conditions in which the nature, quality, and price of goods and services are determined by competitive market forces. In addition to benefiting consumers and a jurisdiction's economy as a whole, such a competitive environment rewards enterprises that respond efficiently to consumer demand. Enterprises can contribute to this process by providing information and advice when governments are considering laws and policies that might reduce efficiency or otherwise reduce the competitiveness of markets.

119. Enterprises should be aware that competition laws continue to be enacted, and that it is increasingly common for those laws to prohibit anti-competitive activities that occur abroad if they have a harmful impact on domestic consumers. Moreover, cross-border trade and investment makes it more likely that anti-competitive conduct taking place in one jurisdiction will have harmful effects in other jurisdictions. Enterprises should therefore take into account both the law of the country in which they are operating and the laws of all countries in which the effects of their conduct are likely to be felt.

120. Finally, enterprises should recognise that competition authorities are engaging in more and deeper co-operation in investigating and challenging anti-competitive activity. See generally: relevant OECD standards in the area of competition policy. When the competition authorities of various jurisdictions are reviewing the same conduct, enterprises' facilitation of co-operation among the authorities promotes consistent and sound decision-making and competitive remedies while also permitting cost savings for governments and enterprises.

121. While enterprises and the collaborative initiatives in which they are involved should take proactive steps to understand competition law issues in their jurisdiction and avoid activities which could represent a breach of competition law, credible responsible business conduct initiatives are not inherently in tension with the purposes of competition law and typically collaboration in such initiatives will not be in breach of such laws.

122. Depending on national context, enterprises may be subject to competition law when buying labour input from workers in a similar way as when buying other goods and services. In these instances, severe sanctions may be applied in the case of collusion between employers on salaries (wage-fixing) and hiring practices (such as no-poach and no-hiring agreements). Enterprises should therefore ensure they comply with applicable laws in their recruitment and employment policies, and when planning mergers and acquisitions.

XI. Taxation

1. It is important that enterprises contribute to the public finances of host countries by making timely payment of their tax liabilities. In particular, enterprises should comply with both the letter and spirit of the tax laws and regulations of the countries in which they operate. Complying with the spirit of the law means discerning and following the intention of the legislature. It does not require an enterprise to make payment in excess of the amount legally required pursuant to such an interpretation. Tax compliance includes such measures as providing to the relevant authorities timely information that is relevant or required by law for purposes of the correct determination of taxes to be assessed in connection with their operations and conforming transfer pricing practices to the arm's length principle.
2. Enterprises should treat tax governance and tax compliance as important elements of their oversight and broader risk management systems. In particular, corporate boards should adopt tax risk management strategies to ensure that the financial, regulatory and reputational risks associated with taxation are fully identified and evaluated.

Commentary on Chapter XI: Taxation

123. Corporate citizenship in the area of taxation implies that enterprises should comply with both the letter and the spirit of the tax laws and regulations in all countries in which they operate, co-operate with authorities and make information that is relevant or required by law available to them. An enterprise complies with the spirit of the tax laws and regulations if it takes reasonable steps to determine the intention of the legislature and interprets those tax rules consistent with that intention in light of the statutory language and relevant, contemporaneous legislative history. Transactions should not be structured in a way that will have tax results that are inconsistent with the underlying economic consequences of the transaction unless there exists specific legislation designed to give that result. In this case, the enterprise should reasonably believe that the transaction is structured in a way that gives a tax result for the enterprise which is not contrary to the intentions of the legislature.

124. Tax compliance also entails co-operation with tax authorities and provision of the information they require to ensure an effective and equitable application of the tax laws. Such co-operation should include responding in a timely and complete manner to requests for information made by a competent authority pursuant to the provisions of a tax treaty or exchange of information agreement. However, this commitment to provide information is not without limitation. In particular, the *Guidelines* make a link between the information that should be provided and its relevance to the enforcement of applicable tax laws. This recognises the need to balance the burden on business in complying with applicable tax laws and the need for tax authorities to have the complete, timely and accurate information to enable them to enforce their tax laws.

125. Enterprises' commitments to co-operation, transparency and tax compliance should be reflected in risk management systems, structures and policies. In the case of enterprises having a corporate legal form, corporate boards are in a position to oversee tax risk in a number of ways. For example, corporate boards should proactively develop appropriate tax policy principles, as well as establish internal tax control systems so that the actions of management are consistent with the views of the board with regard to tax

risk. The board should be informed about all potentially material tax risks and responsibility should be assigned for performing internal tax control functions and reporting to the board. A comprehensive risk management strategy that includes tax will allow the enterprise to not only act as a good corporate citizen but also to effectively manage tax risk, which can serve to avoid major financial, regulatory and reputation risk for an enterprise.

126. Tax transparency supports the integrity of a country's tax system and is an important way of ensuring and demonstrating that enterprises comply with the letter and spirit of tax laws. A member of a multinational enterprise group in one country may have extensive economic relationships with members of the same multinational enterprise group in other countries. Such relationships may affect the tax liability of each of the parties. Accordingly, tax authorities may need information from outside their jurisdiction in order to be able to evaluate those relationships and determine the tax liability of the member of the multinational enterprise group in their jurisdiction. Again, the information to be provided is limited to that which is relevant to or required by law for the proposed evaluation of those economic relationships for the purpose of determining the correct tax liability of the member of the multinational enterprise group. Multinational enterprises should co-operate in providing that information. A number of actions of the *OECD/G20 Inclusive Framework on Base Erosion and Profit Shifting (BEPS)* project are aimed at improving transparency, such as the preparation and exchange of Country-by-Country Reports (BEPS Action 13), the compulsory spontaneous exchange of relevant information on taxpayer-specific rulings (BEPS Action 5), and the mandatory disclosure rules regarding aggressive tax planning schemes (BEPS Action 12).

127. Transfer pricing is a particularly important issue for corporate citizenship and taxation. The dramatic increase in global trade and cross-border direct investment (and the important role played in such trade and investment by multinational enterprises) means that transfer pricing is a significant determinant of the tax liabilities of members of a multinational enterprise group because it materially influences the division of the tax base between countries in which the multinational enterprise operates. The arm's length principle which is included in both the OECD Model Tax Convention and the UN Model Double Taxation Convention between Developed and Developing Countries, is the internationally accepted standard for adjusting the profits between associated enterprises. Application of the arm's length principle avoids inappropriate shifting of profits or losses and minimises risks of double taxation. Its proper application requires multinational enterprises to co-operate with tax authorities and to furnish all information that is relevant or required by law regarding the selection of the transfer pricing method adopted for the international transactions undertaken by them and their related party. It is recognised that determining whether transfer pricing adequately reflects the arm's length standard (or principle) is often difficult both for multinational enterprises and for tax administrations and that its application is not an exact science.

128. The Committee on Fiscal Affairs of the OECD undertakes ongoing work to develop recommendations for ensuring that transfer pricing reflects the arm's length principle. Its work resulted in the publication in 1995 of the *OECD Transfer Pricing Guidelines for Multinational Enterprises and Tax Administrations (OECD Transfer Pricing Guidelines) which was the subject of the Recommendation on the Determination of Transfer Pricing between Associated Enterprises [OECD/LEGAL/0279]* (members of a multinational enterprise group would normally fall within the definition of Associated Enterprises). The *OECD Transfer Pricing Guidelines* are updated on an ongoing basis to reflect changes in the global economy and experiences of tax administrations and taxpayers dealing with transfer pricing. Importantly, the Council Recommendation was revised in 2017 to reflect the endorsement by the Council of the BEPS package, to strengthen the impact and relevance of the Transfer Pricing Guidelines outside OECD Membership, and to provide greater clarity and legal certainty to governments and taxpayers on the status of future revisions to the Transfer Pricing Guidelines by supporting their timely implementation. The arm's length principle as it applies to the attribution of profits of permanent establishments for the purposes of the determination of a host State's taxing rights under a tax treaty was the subject of an OECD Council Recommendation adopted in 2008.

129. The *OECD Transfer Pricing Guidelines* focus on the application of the arm's length principle to evaluate the transfer pricing of associated enterprises. The OECD Transfer Pricing Guidelines aim to help tax administrations (of both OECD member countries and non-member countries) and multinational enterprises by indicating mutually satisfactory solutions to transfer pricing cases, thereby minimising conflict among tax administrations and between tax administrations and multinational enterprises and avoiding costly litigation. Multinational enterprises are encouraged to follow the guidance in the *OECD Transfer Pricing Guidelines*, as revised and supplemented, in order to ensure that their transfer prices reflect the arm's length principle.

130. The coherence and consistency of the international tax architecture that applies to multinational enterprise groups was more broadly reinforced through the OECD/G20 BEPS Project. Notably the *Multilateral Convention to Implement Tax Treaty Related Measures to Prevent Base Erosion and Profit Shifting [OECD/LEGAL/0432]* facilitates implementation of a number of measures to tackle tax avoidance and to improve the coherence of international tax rules, including minimum standards for the avoidance of treaty abuse and for the improvement of dispute resolution. The success of this system is premised on a network of positive relationships, co-operation and reciprocity.

Part II: Implementation Procedures of the OECD Guidelines for Multinational Enterprises on Responsible Business Conduct

Decision of the Council on the Guidelines for Multinational Enterprises on Responsible Business Conduct

THE COUNCIL,

HAVING REGARD to Article 5 a) of the *Convention on the Organisation for Economic Co-operation and Development* of 14 December 1960;

HAVING REGARD to the *OECD Declaration on International Investment and Multinational Enterprises* (the "*Declaration*") *[OECD/LEGAL/0144],* in which the Members and non-Members having adhered ("Adherents") jointly recommend to multinational enterprises operating in or from their territories the observance of *Guidelines for Multinational Enterprises on Responsible Business Conduct* (the "*Guidelines*");

RECOGNISING that, since operations of multinational enterprises extend throughout the world, international co-operation on issues relating to the Declaration should extend to all countries;

CONSIDERING it desirable to enhance procedures by which consultations may take place on matters covered by these *Guidelines* and to promote the effectiveness of the *Guidelines*;

On the proposal of the Investment Committee:

DECIDES:

I. National Contact Points for Responsible Business Conduct

1. Adherents shall set up National Contact Points for Responsible Business Conduct (NCPs) to further the effectiveness of the *Guidelines*. NCPs shall have the following responsibilities:

   a) Promote awareness and uptake of the *Guidelines*, including by responding to enquiries;
   b) Contribute to the resolution of issues that arise in relation to the implementation of the *Guidelines* in specific instances.

In addition, where appropriate and in coordination with relevant government agencies, NCPs may also provide support to efforts by their government to develop, implement, and foster coherence of policies to promote responsible business conduct.

The business community, worker organisations, other non-governmental organisations and other interested parties shall be informed of the availability of NCPs.

2. NCPs in different Adherents shall co-operate, if such need arises, on any matter related to the *Guidelines* relevant to their activities. As a general procedure, discussions at the national level should be initiated before contacts with other NCPs are undertaken.

3. NCPs shall meet regularly to share experiences and report to the Investment Committee.

4. Adherents shall make available human and financial resources to their NCPs so that they can effectively fulfil their responsibilities in a way that fully meets the effectiveness criteria described in the Procedures attached to this Decision, taking into account internal budget capacity and practices.

5. Adherents shall undertake periodic peer reviews of their NCPs, subject to modalities adopted by the Working Party on Responsible Business Conduct (WPRBC).

II. The Investment Committee and the Working Party on Responsible Business Conduct

1. The Investment Committee ("the Committee") shall oversee the implementation of the Declaration on International Investment and Multinational Enterprises. The WPRBC shall assist the Committee in implementing Section I of the Declaration with respect to its responsibilities in relation to the Guidelines.

2. The Committee shall periodically or at the request of an Adherent hold exchanges of views on matters covered by the *Guidelines* and the experience gained in their application. The Committee shall periodically invite Business at OECD (BIAC), the Trade Union Advisory Committee to the OECD (TUAC) (the "advisory bodies"), and OECD Watch, as well as other international partners to express their views on matters covered by the *Guidelines*. In addition, exchanges of views with them on these matters may be held at their request.

3. The Committee shall engage with non-Adherents on matters covered by the *Guidelines* in order to promote responsible business conduct worldwide in accordance with the *Guidelines* and to create a level playing field. It shall also strive to co-operate with non-Adherents that have a special interest in the *Guidelines* and in promoting their principles and standards.

4. The Committee shall be responsible for clarification of the *Guidelines*. Parties involved in a specific instance that gave rise to a request for clarification shall be given the opportunity to express their views either orally or in writing. The Committee shall not reach conclusions on the conduct of individual enterprises.

5. The Committee shall hold exchanges of views on the activities of NCPs with a view to enhancing the effectiveness of the *Guidelines* and fostering functional equivalence of NCPs.

6. The Committee shall periodically report to the Council on matters covered by the *Guidelines*. In its reports, the Committee shall take account of reports by NCPs and the views expressed by the advisory bodies (BIAC and TUAC), OECD Watch, other international partners and non-Adherents as appropriate.

7. The Committee shall, in co-operation with NCPs, proactively promote the effective observance by enterprises of the principles and standards contained in the *Guidelines*. It shall, in particular, seek opportunities to collaborate with the advisory bodies (BIAC and TUAC), OECD Watch, other international partners and other stakeholders in order to encourage positive contributions from multinational enterprises, in the context of the *Guidelines*, to economic, environmental and social progress with a view to achieving sustainable development, and to help identify and respond to risks of adverse impacts associated with particular products, regions, sectors or industries.

III. Implementation and Review of the Decision

1. The Procedures attached to this Decision set out expectations, recommendations and guidance applicable to Adherents, NCPs, the Committee, and the WPRBC in the implementation of this Decision.

2. This Decision shall be periodically reviewed. The Committee shall make proposals for this purpose, and the WPRBC may develop and submit such proposals to the Committee.

Procedures

I. National Contact Points for Responsible Business Conduct

The role of National Contact Points for Responsible Business Conduct (NCPs) is to further the effectiveness of the *Guidelines*. NCPs will operate in a manner that is:

1. visible,
2. accessible,
3. transparent,
4. accountable,
5. impartial and equitable,
6. predictable, and
7. compatible with the *Guidelines*.

These principles together comprise the core effectiveness criteria of NCPs. NCPs, considering their particular circumstances, will pursue functional equivalence, meaning that all NCPs function with an equivalent degree of effectiveness, through achieving the core effectiveness criteria.

A. Institutional Arrangements

Consistent with the objectives of functional equivalence of NCPs and furthering the effectiveness of the *Guidelines*, Adherents have flexibility in organising their NCPs to meet the core effectiveness criteria. In determining the institutional arrangements of their NCP, governments will seek the active support of social partners where applicable, and other stakeholders as well as other relevant government agencies.

Accordingly, the NCPs:

1. Will be composed, organised, and sufficiently resourced to provide an effective basis for dealing with the broad range of issues covered by the *Guidelines*, have access to expertise on all relevant aspects of the NCP mandate, operate in an impartial manner and maintain an adequate level of accountability to the adhering government.
2. Can use different forms of organisation to meet the core effectiveness criteria and pursue functional equivalence, keeping in mind the importance of maintaining stakeholder confidence. For example, an NCP can consist of a senior government official or a government office headed by a senior official; an interagency or inter-ministerial body composed of, or led by, senior officials; a body composed of representatives from the government, the business community, worker organisations and other non-governmental organisations (multi-stakeholder), and/or independent experts. Governments are encouraged to include representatives of the business community, worker organisations and other non-governmental organisations in advisory or oversight bodies where useful to assist the NCP in its tasks.
3. Will develop and maintain meaningful relations and engage with social partners where applicable, as well as representatives of the business community, worker organisations, non-governmental

organisations, and/or other interested parties that are able to contribute to the effectiveness of the *Guidelines*.

B. Information and Promotion

The NCP will:

1. Make the *Guidelines* known and available by appropriate means, including through on-line information, and in national languages. NCPs should also promote related OECD due diligence guidance on responsible business conduct, taking into account the specific nature of the guidance as mentioned in the *Guidelines* Chapter II, Commentary paragraph 15. Relevant stakeholders, including prospective investors (inward and outward), should be informed about the *Guidelines*, as appropriate.
2. Raise awareness of the *Guidelines*, their implementation procedures, and the NCP itself, including through co-operation, as appropriate, with relevant government agencies, the business community, worker organisations, other non-governmental organisations, and the interested public.
3. Respond to enquiries about the *Guidelines* and OECD due diligence guidance, as well as the NCP itself, including from:
    a) other NCPs;
    b) the business community, worker organisations, other non-governmental organisations and the public; and
    c) governments of non-Adherents.

C. Specific Instances

The NCP will, serving as a non-judicial grievance mechanism, contribute to the resolution of issues that arise relating to the implementation of the *Guidelines* in specific instances in a manner that is consistent with the core effectiveness criteria listed in Section I.A. above. NCPs will publish their case-handling procedures, i.e. procedures they follow in handling specific instances, which will be consistent with these Procedures. NCPs are encouraged to consult their stakeholders in developing their case-handling procedures. The NCP will offer a forum for discussion and its expertise on the *Guidelines* to assist the business community, worker organisations, other non-governmental organisations, and other interested parties concerned to resolve the issues raised in an efficient and timely manner and in accordance with applicable law and the *Guidelines*. Depending on the characteristics of each case, this assistance may include supporting constructive dialogue, facilitating agreements between the parties and/or issuing recommendations. The aims of such assistance may include furthering the implementation of the Guidelines in the future and/or addressing adverse impacts in a way consistent with the *Guidelines.*

In providing this assistance, the NCP will:

1. Where other NCPs are concerned due to the characteristics of the Specific Instance, coordinate in good faith with them to choose the lead and supporting NCPs.
2. Consult the parties on the issues raised and make an initial assessment of whether these issues warrant further examination and respond to the parties involved.
3. Where, based on an initial assessment, the NCP decides that the issues raised warrant further examination, offer good offices to help the parties involved to resolve the issues. For this purpose, the NCP will consult with these parties and where relevant:
    a) seek advice from relevant authorities, and/or representatives of the business community, worker organisations, other non-governmental organisations, and relevant experts;
    b) consult the NCP or NCPs in any other Adherent or Adherents concerned;
    c) seek information on similar specific instances from the Secretariat or guidance from the WPRBC if it has doubt about the interpretation of the *Guidelines*. Such information and

guidance is advisory, confidential and case-specific and does not amount to clarifications of the interpretation of the *Guidelines*, which remain the responsibility of the Committee as per Section II.2.c) below. Subject to available resources, it should be provided expeditiously to avoid delays in the handling of the case;

d) offer and, with the agreement of the parties involved, facilitate access to consensual and non-adversarial means, such as mediation or conciliation, to assist the parties in resolving the issues.

4. At the conclusion of the proceedings and after consultation with the parties involved, make the results of the proceedings publicly available, taking into account the need to protect sensitive business and other stakeholder information, by publicly issuing a final statement:

   a) when the NCP decides that the issues raised do not warrant further examination. The statement should at a minimum describe the issues raised, the parties' respective positions as appropriate, the steps taken by the NCP in considering the submission and parties' engagement in the proceedings, and the reasons for the NCP's decision;

   b) when the parties have reached agreement on the issues raised. The statement should at a minimum describe the issues raised, the parties' respective positions as appropriate, the steps taken by the NCP in assisting the parties and when agreement was reached. Information on the content of the agreement will only be included insofar as the parties involved agree thereto. The NCP may also include recommendations on the implementation of the *Guidelines* in its statements when an agreement has been reached, as appropriate;

   c) when no agreement is reached or when a party is unwilling to participate in the proceedings. This statement should at a minimum describe the issues raised, the parties' respective positions as appropriate, the reasons why the NCP decided that the issues raised warranted further examination and the steps taken by the NCP in assisting the parties, including information on parties' engagement in the proceedings. The NCP should also include recommendations on the implementation of the *Guidelines* where relevant. Where appropriate, the statement could also include the reasons why an agreement could not be reached. If allowed by applicable law and the NCP's case-handling procedures, the NCP may, at its own discretion, set out its views in its final statement on whether the enterprise observed the *Guidelines.*

   The NCP will notify the results of its specific instances to the Committee and the WPRBC in a timely manner.

5. Engage in follow-up where relevant once the specific instance has closed, on the implementation of recommendations or, if any, the agreement reached by the parties. The NCP should publish a follow up statement. Any follow up that the NCP intends to undertake should also be referred to in the final statement, including deadlines to do so.

6. Act with transparency and make parties to a specific instance aware of all relevant facts and arguments brought to the NCP by other parties, in particular during the good offices phase. However, upon a reasonable request by a party, for example to protect sensitive information and/or the interests of stakeholders involved in the specific instance the NCP may keep certain information confidential from the other parties.

7. Inform the parties that they may not disclose publicly or to a third party, during or after the proceedings, facts and arguments shared by the other parties or the NCP (including where relevant by an external mediator or conciliator) during the proceedings described in paragraphs 1-5 above, unless the sharing party agrees to their disclosure, such facts and arguments are already in the public domain, or not disclosing would be contrary to the provisions of national law.

8. If issues arise in non-Adherents, take steps to develop an understanding of the issues involved, and follow these Procedures.

9. Throughout the process, NCPs should take all appropriate steps within their capacities to address risks of reprisals against parties to a specific instance. If they become aware of an actual or potential instance of reprisal, NCPs should, to the extent possible, support the party concerned in avoiding and mitigating any harm and contact relevant authorities, in consultation with the person(s) at risk where possible. Governments should also take relevant steps to protect the NCP and its members from reprisals.

D. Support for government efforts to promote responsible business conduct

In furthering the effectiveness of the Guidelines, NCPs may, where appropriate and in coordination with relevant government agencies, support efforts by their government to develop, implement, and foster coherence of policies aimed at promoting responsible business conduct. Providing or requesting such support should take into account the NCP's resources and capacity to fulfil their responsibilities described in paragraph I.1. of the *Decision*.

E. Reporting

1. Each NCP will report annually to the Committee and the WPRBC.
2. Reports should contain information on the nature and results of the activities of the NCP, including in specific instances.

F. Peer reviews

Adherents will undertake periodic peer reviews of their NCP organised by the Secretariat, as a means to increase effective implementation of the *Guidelines*, share best practices, and foster NCP effectiveness and functional equivalence. Modalities for periodic peer reviews, including procedures for conducting peer reviews, the duration of the peer review cycle and funding arrangements, will be approved by the WPRBC and reviewed at the end of every cycle. The first cycle of periodic peer reviews will only be launched after such modalities have been approved.

II. Investment Committee, WPRBC and the Secretariat

1. The Committee, the WPRBC and the Secretariat will consider requests from NCPs for assistance in carrying out their activities, including in the event of doubt about the interpretation of the *Guidelines* in particular circumstances, each in accordance with their respective responsibilities.

2. The Committee, with the assistance of the WPRBC, will, with a view to enhance the effectiveness of the *Guidelines* and to foster the functional equivalence of NCPs:

a) consider the annual reports of NCPs described in Section I.E. above. Based on such reports, the WPRBC will annually issue a public report analysing the activities of NCPs;

b) consider a substantiated submission by an Adherent, an advisory body (BIAC or TUAC) or OECD Watch on whether an NCP is fulfilling its responsibilities with regard to its handling of specific instances. The Committee will approve the response by consensus. The Adherent whose NCP is the subject of a substantiated submission will participate in the process in good faith, and is expected to join the consensus except in exceptional circumstances;

c) consider issuing a clarification of the interpretation of the Guidelines at the request of an Adherent, an advisory body (BIAC or TUAC) or OECD Watch. Such request may concern whether an NCP has correctly interpreted the *Guidelines* in specific instances, but in such cases, the Committee will not reach conclusions on the conduct of individual enterprises;

d) make recommendations, as necessary, to improve the functioning of NCPs and the effective implementation of the *Guidelines*. When, based on the last two annual reporting cycles and upon proposal by the WPRBC, the Committee determines that an NCP has, for an extended period of time and without legitimate reason, manifestly not been operating in a way consistent with these *Procedures*, it may make appropriate recommendations to the Adherent and invite it to report back within a set timeframe, and the Committee may do so repeatedly until it is satisfied that the issues have been addressed. The Committee and the WPRBC will reach decisions on these matters by consensus. The Adherent whose NCP is concerned will participate in the process in good faith, and is expected to join the consensus except in exceptional circumstances;

e) co-operate with international partners;

f) engage with interested non-Adherents on matters covered by the *Guidelines* and their implementation.

3. The Committee and the WPRBC may seek and consider advice from experts on any matters covered by the *Guidelines*. For this purpose, the Committee will decide on suitable procedures.

4. The Committee and the WPRBC will discharge their responsibilities in an efficient and timely manner.

5. In discharging their responsibilities, the Committee and the WPRBC will be assisted by the Secretariat, which, under the overall guidance of the Committee and the WPRBC, and subject to the Organisation's Programme of Work and Budget, will:

a) serve as a central point of information for NCPs that have questions on the promotion, interpretation, and implementation of the *Guidelines*. Information on the interpretation of the Guidelines will be provided in accordance with I.C.2.c) above;

b) collect and make publicly available – including by supporting the WPRBC with the publication of the annual report analysing NCP activities under II. 2. a) above – relevant information on recent trends and emerging practices with regard to NCPs' institutional arrangements, promotional activities and the implementation of the *Guidelines* in specific instances. The Secretariat will develop unified reporting formats to support the establishment and maintenance of an up-to-date database on specific instances and conduct regular analysis of these specific instances;

c) facilitate peer learning activities, as well as capacity building and training, in particular for NCPs of new Adherents and new NCP personnel, on the *Guidelines* and their Implementation Procedures such as promotion and the facilitation of conciliation and mediation;

d) organise periodic peer reviews of NCPs as indicated under Section I.F. above;

e) facilitate co-operation between NCPs where appropriate; and

f) promote the *Guidelines* in relevant international forums and meetings and provide support to NCPs and the Committee in their efforts to raise awareness of the *Guidelines* among non-Adherents.

III. Miscellaneous

These Procedures do not give rise to additional rights or obligations under international law.

Commentaries on the Implementation Procedures

1. The Council Decision represents the commitment of Adherents to further the implementation of the recommendations contained in the text of the *Guidelines*. Procedures are attached to the Council Decision and outline expectations, recommendations, and other guidance for Adherents, National Contact Points for Responsible Business Conduct (NCPs), the Investment Committee (the Committee), the Working Party on Responsible Business Conduct (WPRBC) and the Secretariat, without giving rise to additional rights or obligations under international law. Expectations are signalled using 'will'. Recommendations are signalled by 'should' or 'encourage'. Guidance is signalled by 'may' or 'can'.

2. The Council Decision sets out key Adherent responsibilities for the Guidelines with respect to NCPs, summarised as follows:

- Setting up NCPs and informing interested parties of the availability of *Guidelines*-related facilities.
- Making available necessary human and financial resources.
- Enabling NCPs in different Adherents to co-operate with each other as necessary.
- Enabling NCPs to meet regularly and report to the Committee.

3. The Council Decision also establishes the Committee's responsibilities for the *Guidelines*, including:

- Organising exchanges of views on matters relating to the *Guidelines*.
- Issuing clarifications as necessary.
- Holding exchanges of views on the activities of NCPs.
- Reporting to the OECD Council on the *Guidelines*.

4. The Investment Committee is the OECD body responsible for overseeing the functioning of the *Guidelines*. This responsibility applies not only to the *Guidelines*, but to all elements of the Declaration (National Treatment Instrument, and the instruments on International Investment Incentives and Disincentives, and Conflicting Requirements). The Committee seeks to ensure that each element in the Declaration is respected and understood, and that they all complement and operate in harmony with each other.

5. The WPRBC is a subsidiary body of the Committee with responsibilities in relation to the *Guidelines* and the Decision. The Procedures list a number of ways in which the WPRBC provides assistance to the Committee, including:

- Developing modalities for periodic peer reviews of NCPs, overseeing the organisation of the peer reviews by the Secretariat, and approving peer review reports;
- Providing advisory guidance to NCPs who have questions regarding the interpretation of the *Guidelines* in particular circumstances;
- Preparing Committee responses on substantiated submissions and requests for clarification of the *Guidelines*;

- Advising the Committee on making recommendations to an Adherent whose NCP has become manifestly non-functioning for an extended period of time and without legitimate reason;
- Supporting the Committee with considering annual reports of NCPs and issuing an annual public report on NCP activity.

6. Reflecting the increasing relevance of responsible business conduct to non-Adherents, the Decision provides for engagement and co-operation with non-Adherents on matters covered by the *Guid*elines. This provision allows the Committee to arrange special meetings with interested non-Adherents to promote understanding of the standards and principles contained in the Guidelines and of their implementation procedures. Subject to relevant OECD procedures, the Committee may also associate them with special activities or projects on responsible business conduct, including by inviting them to its meetings.

7. The Committee will co-operate with NCPs and seek opportunities to collaborate with the advisory bodies (BIAC and TUAC), OECD Watch, and other international partners with the objective of proactively promoting effective implementation of the Guidelines. In particular, as part of its work to oversee the implementation of the Declaration, the Committee, with the support of the WPRBC, will provide guidance on, and seek to enhance the capacity of business to implement, due diligence for responsible business conduct, including in specific sectors, geographies and risk areas. It will be conducted through, *inter alia*, multi-stakeholder engagement and take into account the needs of small- and medium-sized enterprises, in co-operation with the NCPs. Further guidance for NCPs in this respect is provided in paragraph 21 below.

I. Commentary on the Procedures for NCPs

8. NCPs have an important role in enhancing the profile and effectiveness of the *Guidelines*. While it is enterprises that are responsible for observing the *Guidelines* in their day-to-day behaviour, governments and their NCPs can contribute to improving the effective implementation of the *Guidelines*. To this end, they have agreed that better direction for the organisation and activities of NCPs is warranted, including through regular meetings and Committee oversight.

9. Many of the functions and activities in the Procedures of the Decision are not new, but reflect experience and recommendations developed over the years. By making them explicit, the expected functioning of the implementation mechanisms of the *Guidelines* is made more transparent. All functions are now outlined in six parts of the Procedures pertaining to NCPs: institutional arrangements, information and promotion, specific instances, support for government efforts to promote responsible business conduct, reporting, and peer reviews.

10. These six parts are preceded by an introductory paragraph that sets out the basic purpose of NCPs, together with the core effectiveness criteria. While governments are accorded flexibility in the way they organise NCPs, NCPs should all function with an equivalent degree of effectiveness, defined as 'functional equivalence'. Functional equivalence is crucial to the effective contribution of the entire NCP network to the implementation of the *Guidelines,* in particular with regard to the full involvement of all NCPs in the specific instance mechanism. Such involvement by all NCPs is important for stakeholder confidence and the full effectiveness of NCPs across the board. All NCPs, each in light of their particular circumstances, will pursue functional equivalence through achieving the core effectiveness criteria described below in the delivery of their responsibilities, which will also assist the Committee and the WPRBC in peer reviews and in discussing the conduct of NCPs.

Core Effectiveness Criteria for Functional Equivalence in the Activities of NCPs:

a. Visible.

In conformity with the Decision, Adherents agree to set up NCPs that are easily identifiable by stakeholders and relevant government agencies within and outside their country, and also to inform the business community, worker organisations and other interested parties, including NGOs, about the availability of facilities associated with NCPs in the implementation of the *Guidelines*. As a basic step in this respect, NCPs will have a comprehensive website or webpage. Governments are expected to publish information about their NCPs, such as its location in government, institutional arrangements and case-handling procedures, and to take an active role in promoting the *Guidelines*, which could include promotional events and materials on the instrument. These events or materials could be prepared in co-operation with business, labour, NGOs, and other interested parties, though not necessarily with all groups on each occasion.

b. Accessible.

Easy access to NCPs is important to their effective functioning. This includes facilitating access by business, labour, NGOs, and other members of the public. NCPs should respond to all legitimate requests for information, and also undertake to handle specific instances in an efficient and timely manner. NCPs will not charge a submission fee and requirements to file a case will be clearly stated, readily available, and not unnecessarily burdensome. Where appropriate and commensurate with the NCP's time and budget capacity, NCPs may also provide impartial and equitable assistance to the parties involved. Such assistance may concern, for example, the use of languages and translations, guidance on presenting an admissible submission and engaging in mediation, allowing flexibility regarding deadlines, or providing affordable options for participation in the process, such as remote meeting facilities.

c. Transparent.

Transparency is an important criterion with respect to its contribution to the other core effectiveness criteria, and in gaining the confidence of stakeholders, parties to specific instances and the general public. Thus, as a general principle and subject to applicable law, the activities of the NCP will be transparent. For example, publishing the annual reports of NCPs to the OECD can demonstrate transparency. Nonetheless in specific instances, the NCP may establish confidentiality of certain aspects of the proceedings, consistent with Section I.C.6.-7. of the Procedures and related Commentary.

d. Accountable.

In light of their role to enhance the profile of the *Guidelines* – and their potential to aid in the management of difficult issues between enterprises and the societies in which they operate – NCPs will account for their activities. Nationally, parliaments, governments, advisory bodies of NCPs where they exist, as well as stakeholders, could have a role to play in providing feedback on the activities of NCPs and act as a source of continuous learning to improve the performance of NCPs. Annual reports, and regular meetings of NCPs, peer learning activities and peer reviews will provide an opportunity to share experiences and encourage "best practices" with respect to NCPs. The Committee and the WPRBC will also hold exchanges of views and experiences, where the effectiveness of the activities of NCPs could be assessed.

e. Impartial and equitable.

Being impartial and equitable are prerequisites for the continued confidence of stakeholders, parties to specific instances and the general public. Accordingly, governments will organise their NCPs in a way that allows them to act and be perceived as such. NCPs will ensure impartiality in the resolution of specific instances, including by actively seeking to prevent and address potential or perceived conflicts of interests of any person playing a role on behalf of the NCP in assisting the parties with the resolution of issues raised in a specific instance. NCPs should also seek to ensure, notably through clear and accessible case-handling procedures, that the parties can engage in the process on fair and equitable terms, for example by seeking to ensure that power and resource imbalances do not prevent the parties from effectively engaging in the process, or by providing reasonable access to sources of information relevant to the procedure.

f. Predictable.

NCPs' operations will provide clear and publicly available information on their role and the procedures they follow in fulfilling their responsibilities, particularly in the resolution of specific instances. Areas where such information should be provided include:

- the provision of good offices,
- the stages of the specific instance process including indicative timeframes and criteria for initial assessment,
- expectations of good faith and confidentiality,
- the nature of the process and its possible outcomes, and
- the role NCPs can play in monitoring the implementation of agreements reached between the parties or recommendations made by the NCP.

NCPs will publish case-handling procedures drafted in clear and accessible terms, and regularly inform parties to specific instances of the progress of the case, especially where indicative time frames set out in paragraphs 51 and 52 below need to be extended.

g. Compatible with the *Guidelines*.

NCPs will operate in a way that is compatible with the Guidelines. When handling specific instances, this notably means working with parties to avoid any situation where agreements are contrary to the Guidelines, or where case-handling procedures are inconsistent with the Procedures.

Institutional Arrangements

11. NCP institutional arrangements will enable the NCP to meet the core effectiveness criteria, retain the confidence of social partners where applicable, and other stakeholders, and foster the public profile of the *Guidelines*. The Decision and the Procedures afford Adherents flexibility in deciding on their NCP's institutional arrangements, identifying some of the various possible options. They also list minimal features necessary to meet these expectations, such as involving senior leadership, having sufficient human and financial resources, and having sufficient access to expertise on the issues covered by the *Guidelines*. Governments have flexibility to use a different name for their NCP as appropriate for their national context. To foster confidence in the NCP, governments should consult stakeholders regarding decisions that may significantly affect an NCP's institutional arrangements.

12. Regardless of the structure governments have chosen for their NCP, they are encouraged to establish multi-stakeholder advisory or oversight bodies where useful to assist NCPs in their tasks.

13. Adequate resources are essential for the effectiveness and authority of NCPs. The Decision requires Adherents to provide their NCPs with the human and financial resources necessary for the NCP to effectively deliver on its responsibilities in a way that fully meets the effectiveness criteria. Adherents are encouraged to make such resources available to NCPs as part of a dedicated budget where appropriate. In case of staff rotation, Adherents should provide for continuity. This can include providing proper training to new personnel, as needed and with the support of the Secretariat, and preserving institutional memory.

14. NCPs, whatever their composition, will develop and maintain meaningful relations and engage with representatives of relevant government agencies, the business community, worker organisations, other non-governmental organisations, and other interested parties, to gain the active support and confidence of stakeholders.

Information and Promotion

15. The NCP functions associated with information and promotion are fundamentally important to enhancing the profile and awareness of the Guidelines with stakeholders and the general public, and encouraging enterprises to act consistently with the Guidelines and use the OECD due diligence guidance in doing so.

16. NCPs are required to actively promote the Guidelines, and are encouraged to promote the OECD due diligence guidance where relevant, notably as recommended in the Council Recommendations on such guidance, and taking into account the specific nature of the Guidance as mentioned in the Guidelines Chapter II, Commentary paragraph 15. Examples of promotion activities include the provision of materials for stakeholders, or the organisation or participation in events on responsible business conduct. Events related to responsible business conduct organised by the OECD, other NCPs or relevant actors could also be promoted. Promotion activities by the NCP and related information should be easily accessible, available online and by other appropriate means, including in national languages. Links to the Guidelines and OECD due diligence guidance on responsible business conduct on the NCP website should be included. English and French language versions will be available from the OECD Secretariat.

17. As appropriate, NCPs will seek to offer the abovementioned activities and information in an equitable manner to a diverse and representative range of relevant stakeholders. The Procedures mention prospective investors, both inward and outward, as an example. NCPs are also encouraged to reach out to relevant government agencies and diplomatic networks, which can act as important amplifiers to promote the Guidelines and create awareness of the NCP, including with stakeholders in other countries. Depending on an NCP's context and resources, stakeholder mappings and promotional plans may assist in increasing the reach and impact of an NCP's promotional efforts.

18. NCPs should also provide information about their responsibilities and activities in light of the core effectiveness criteria. NCPs should promote their role in specific instances to relevant stakeholders, including, where possible and appropriate, potential submitters of specific instances. This should include information on the process that parties should follow when submitting or responding to a specific instance, advice on the information that is necessary to submit a specific instance, the requirements for parties participating in specific instances, including confidentiality, and the processes and indicative timeframes that will be followed by the NCP.

19. In their efforts to raise awareness of the Guidelines, NCPs will co-operate with a wide variety of organisations and individuals, including, as appropriate, relevant government agencies, the business community, worker organisations, non-governmental organisations, and other interested parties. Such organisations have a strong stake in the promotion of the Guidelines and their institutional networks provide opportunities for promotion that, if used for this purpose, will greatly enhance the efforts of NCPs in this regard.

20. Another basic activity expected of NCPs is responding to legitimate enquiries. Three groups have been singled out for attention in this regard: i) other NCPs (reflecting a provision in the Decision); ii) the business community, worker organisations, other non-governmental organisations and the public; and iii) governments of non-Adherents.

21. To support the Committee and the WPRBC in proactively promoting implementation of the Guidelines, NCPs should maintain regular contact, including meetings, with social partners where applicable and other stakeholders in order to:

a) consider new developments and emerging practices concerning responsible business conduct;
b) support the positive contributions enterprises can make to economic, social and environmental progress;

c) participate where appropriate in collaborative initiatives to identify and respond to risks of ad verse impacts associated with particular products, regions, sectors or industries.

Peer Learning

22. In addition to contributing to the Committee's and the WPRBC's work to enhance the effectiveness of the Guidelines, NCPs will engage in joint peer learning activities. Such peer learning can be carried out through meetings at the OECD or through direct co-operation between NCPs.

Peer Reviews

23. Peer reviews are an important mechanism to increase effective implementation of the *Guidelines*, share best practices, and foster functional equivalence. As set out in the Decision, Adherents commit to undertake periodic peer reviews of the NCPs. The Secretariat will organise such peer reviews under the oversight of the WPRBC. Peer reviews evaluate strengths and weaknesses of the NCP with regard to the delivery of its mandate and the core effectiveness criteria defined in Section I of the Procedures, and make recommendations for improvement as appropriate.

24. The modalities of the periodic peer reviews (process, duration of the review cycle and funding arrangements) will be defined in a 'Core Template for NCP Peer Reviews' to be approved by consensus by the WPRBC and published on the OECD Website. The WPRBC will review the Core Template at the end of each cycle, in particular to ensure that NCPs are given enough time to prepare their peer reviews, that peer reviews do not represent an unreasonable burden, are cost-effective for governments and NCPs (including peer reviewer NCPs) and take into account the workloads of the WPRBC and the Secretariat, and that the selection process for peer reviewer NCPs ensures that all NCPs are offered an opportunity to participate in peer review teams. The cycle of periodic peer reviews will not start until modalities have been approved by the WPRBC.

Specific Instances

25. When issues arise relating to implementation of the *Guidelines* in specific instances, the NCP is expected to assist in resolving them, serving as a non-judicial grievance mechanism. In that context, NCPs will aim to facilitate dialogue between the parties and support them in seeking mutually agreeable and *Guidelines*-compatible solutions to the issues raised, but also actively inform such dialogue with their expertise on the *Guidelines*. NCPs should also draft final statements in such a way as to provide guidance on resolving the issues and implementing the *Guidelines*. OECD Due Diligence Guidance on Responsible Business Conduct and OECD sector due diligence guidances are a useful resource for NCPs in understanding and promoting the *Guidelines* but are not intended to serve as the sole basis for the submission of specific instances. Each NCP will publish clear and easily accessible case-handling procedures outlining its specific instance process consistent with these Procedures. NCP are encouraged to develop their case-handling procedures in consultation with stakeholders.

Good Faith Engagement

26. The specific instance process is voluntary. The good faith engagement by all parties involved in the proceedings is expected. Good faith engagement in this context means responding in a timely fashion, maintaining confidentiality where appropriate and consistent with the NCP's case-handling procedures, refraining from misrepresenting the issues and the process, notably in public communications, and from threatening or taking reprisals against parties involved in the procedure, or against the NCP itself, and genuinely engaging in the proceedings with a view to finding a *Guidelines*-compatible solution to the issues raised, including giving serious consideration to any offer of good offices made by the NCP.

27. Should an NCP become aware of the threat of or existence of reprisals directed at a person involved in a specific instance, or towards the NCP or one of its members, it should take steps within its capacities, and in consultation with other relevant government entities such as diplomatic missions, as appropriate, with the aim of ensuring that the person at risk has adequate protection and that the

proceedings can continue in a safe, accessible, equitable and impartial manner. Before undertaking any action in this regard, the NCP will consult with the person at risk where possible. Reprisals may include threats to harm the individual, their family or other relations, inappropriate threats to terminate employment or benefits or inappropriate threats of legal action. Appropriate measures may include, for example, keeping the identity of the person at risk confidential, suggesting that the person at risk be represented by a trusted third party, documenting attempted reprisals in statements, reaching out to relevant authorities or assisting the person at risk in doing so.

28. Additionally, to preserve accessibility and impartiality, governments should take appropriate steps to protect the NCP and its members from reprisals, in line with domestic law and in consultation with competent government authorities. Governments should support measures taken by the NCP to protect itself and its members.

Coordination between NCPs in Specific Instances

29. As the *Guidelines* are addressed by Adherents to enterprises operating "in or from" their territory, NCPs may receive specific instances regarding issues taking place in their country or alternatively regarding issues concerning enterprises established in their country. Accordingly, certain specific instances may concern the NCPs of several Adherents, such as:

- where a specific instance concerns different home and host adhering countries (e.g. concerning the activities of an enterprise headquartered in one Adherent, having impacts in another Adherent, or an enterprise with different headquarters in multiple Adherents);
- where the issues raised in a specific instance take place in several Adherents, or concern several enterprises established in several Adherents;
- where the same specific instance or related specific instances (such as specific instances involving different enterprises active on the same project or in the same supply chain) are submitted to several NCPs.

In such situations, the NCP(s) that received the specific instance(s) will inform and coordinate with all other concerned NCPs at the outset with the goal of designating the lead and supporting NCPs and adopting coordination arrangements.

30. Generally, the NCP of the country in which the issues have arisen would be the lead NCP. However, in certain situations other criteria may be applied, e.g. when needed in order to contribute to the resolution of the issues raised, or when issues have arisen in a non-Adherent. The parties should be kept informed with regard to coordination arrangements, and consulted on decisions to transfer the case to a different lead NCP than the NCP to which the case was submitted.

31. The lead NCP is responsible for all aspects of the specific instance process and its case-handling procedures will be applicable to the process. Throughout the specific instance process, supporting NCPs will be kept informed of developments and may lend resources by for example reviewing statements/reports, providing translation services, supporting joint meetings with parties, and other practical assistance. Supporting NCPs will act in good faith to foster the resolution of the specific instance and all NCPs involved will respect the confidentiality and appropriate use of information and materials received from other NCPs.

32. The NCPs can seek assistance, including proposals, from the Chair of the WPRBC when discussing the selection of lead and supporting NCPs and the coordination among them. If the NCPs fail to reach consensus, the NCP(s) that received the specific instance(s) should make a final decision on the case in consultation with the other NCPs concerned and keep them informed regularly of the progress of the case.

Initial Assessment

33. After consulting the parties on the issues raised and, where relevant, coordinating with other NCPs concerned to designate a lead NCP in light of paragraphs 29-32 above, the NCP will make an initial assessment of whether the issue raised warrants further examination.

In making this initial assessment, the NCP will take into account:

- the identity of the party concerned and its interest in the matter;
- whether the issue is material, i.e. relevant to the implementation of the *Guidelines;* and substantiated, i.e. supported by sufficient and credible information;
- whether the enterprise is covered by the *Guidelines*;
- whether there seems to be a link between the enterprise's activities and the issue raised in the specific instance;
- the extent to which applicable law and/or parallel proceedings limit the NCP's ability to contribute to the resolution of the issue and/or the implementation of the *Guidelines*, in light of paragraph 35 below;
- whether the examination of the issue would contribute to the purposes and effectiveness of the *Guidelines*.

34. Following its initial assessment, the NCP will respond to the parties concerned. If the NCP decides that the issues do not warrant further examination, it will inform the parties of the reasons for its decision. A decision that a case warrants further examination does not mean that the issues raised have been given final consideration and does not imply any finding as to whether or not an enterprise has acted in accordance with the *Guidelines.*

Parallel proceedings

35. The term "parallel proceedings" refers to judicial or non-judicial processes, which may be domestic or international in nature, involving the same or closely related issues and which could influence the ongoing specific instance. This includes for example specific instances before the same NCP or another NCP. If parallel proceedings have been conducted, are under way or are available to the parties concerned, this does not preclude the NCP from offering good offices to the parties. NCPs should evaluate whether an offer of good offices could make a positive contribution to the resolution of the issues raised and/or the implementation of the *Guidelines* going forward and would not create serious prejudice for either of the parties involved in these other proceedings or cause a contempt of court situation. In making such an evaluation, NCPs could take into account practice among other NCPs, consider the possibility to partially accept the specific instance or to suspend its examination while the parallel proceedings are ongoing and, where appropriate, consult with the institutions in which the parallel proceedings are being or could be conducted. NCPs will seek parties' assistance in considering these matters by requesting relevant information and views on the parallel proceedings.

Good offices

36. Where the issues raised warrant further examination, the NCP will offer "good offices" in an effort to contribute to the resolution of issues. As part of good offices, the NCP may seek the advice of relevant authorities, as well as representatives of the business community, labour organisations, other non-governmental organisations, and experts, consistent with the NCP's own case-handling procedures. Consulting with NCPs in other countries, or seeking information from the Secretariat or guidance from the WPRBC on issues related to the interpretation of the *Guidelines*, may also help to resolve the issue.

37. Through good offices, NCPs will offer a platform for dialogue between the parties to assist with the resolution of the issues raised. In line with the non-judicial nature of the specific instance procedure, and subject to consent of the parties, the role of the NCP includes creating conditions for dialogue and

agreement between the parties around a commitment by the enterprise to further the implementation of the *Guidelines* in the future and, where relevant, address, in accordance with the *Guidelines*, adverse impacts that may have occurred. While facilitating dialogue, the NCP should explain the provisions of the *Guidelines* relevant to the issues raised as a way to support parties in reaching an agreement compatible with the *Guidelines.*

38. As part of making available good offices, and where relevant to the issues at hand, NCPs will offer, or facilitate access to, consensual and non-adversarial processes, such as mediation or conciliation, to assist the parties in resolving issues at hand. In common with accepted practices on conciliation and mediation, these processes would be used only upon agreement of the parties concerned and their commitment to participate in good faith during the procedure. If mediation is the option chosen, NCPs may choose to carry out the mediation themselves or engage external mediators in consultation with the parties to conduct or support mediation.

Conclusion of the Proceedings

39. NCPs are expected to always make the results of a specific instance publicly available in accordance with paragraphs I.C-4. and I.C-6. of the Procedures.

40. When the NCP, after having carried out its initial assessment, decides that the issues raised in the specific instance do not warrant further examination, it will make a statement publicly available after consultations with the parties involved and taking into account the need to preserve the confidentiality of sensitive business and other information. If the NCP believes that, based on the results of its initial assessment, it would be unfair to publicly identify a party in a statement on its decision, it may draft the statement so as to protect the identity of the party.

41. The NCP may also make publicly available its decision that the issues raised warrant further examination and its offer of good offices to the parties involved.

42. If the parties involved reach agreement on the issues raised, the parties should address in their agreement how and to what extent the content of the agreement is to be made publicly available. The NCP, in consultation with the parties, will make publicly available a statement with the results of the proceedings. The NCP can make recommendations on the implementation of the *Guidelines* even if there is agreement or partial agreement between the parties.

43. If the parties involved fail to reach agreement on all or some of the issues raised, if one or both of the parties withdraws from the procedure, or if the NCP finds that one or more of the parties to the specific instance is unwilling to engage or to participate in good faith, the NCP will issue a statement, and make recommendations as appropriate, on the implementation of the *Guidelines* in relation to the issues raised. This procedure makes it clear that an NCP will issue a statement, even when it feels that a specific recommendation is not called for. The statement should identify the parties concerned, the issues involved, the date on which the issues were raised with the NCP, any recommendations by the NCP, and any observations the NCP deems appropriate to include on the reasons why the proceedings did not produce an agreement.

44. Where appropriate and relevant to the resolution of the issues, the NCP may also, at its own discretion, if allowed by applicable national law and its case-handling procedures, set out its views in its final statement on whether the enterprise observed the *Guidelines.* Likewise, where appropriate, the NCP may inform relevant government agencies of the good faith engagement, or absence thereof, of the parties, and should communicate in a transparent manner with the parties about intended or actual steps in this regard.

45. The NCP should provide an opportunity for the parties to comment on a draft statement. However, the statement is that of the NCP and it is within the NCP's discretion to decide whether to change the draft statement in response to comments from the parties.

Follow up

46. NCPs will carry out follow up on agreements they facilitate or recommendations they make where relevant. Follow up may for example not be relevant in situations where parties decline such follow up or agree that the issues have been fully resolved. The deadlines for doing so should be addressed in the statement of the NCP. Follow up may involve, for example, requests for updates from the parties, or one or more meetings between the NCP and the parties (either separately, or together) to assess progress on the implementation of the commitments undertaken in the agreement, or on the NCP's recommendations. The NCP should publish follow up statements after conducting its follow-up.

Transparency and Confidentiality

47. Transparency is recognised as a general principle for the conduct of NCPs (see paragraph 10c. in "Core Effectiveness Criteria" section, above). However, paragraph I.C-6. of the Procedures recognises that there are specific circumstances where maintaining confidentiality of certain facts and arguments brought forward by the parties is justified. For example, the NCP will take appropriate steps to protect sensitive business information, such as commercial secrets. Equally, other information, such as the identity of individuals involved in the proceedings, should be kept confidential, for example if disclosing it places them or related persons at risk of retaliation. Nonetheless, it remains important to strike a balance between transparency and confidentiality in order to build confidence in the specific instance process and to promote the *Guidelines'* effective implementation. It is recognised that NCPs may be obligated to follow national laws on transparency and disclosure, regardless of these provisions.

48. With respect to sharing information between parties, in the interest of an equitable process, the NCP should, in principle, make parties aware of all relevant facts and arguments brought forward to the NCP by the other parties during proceedings (in particular during the good offices phase). If a party makes a reasonable request not to share a submission in full with the other party, notably to protect sensitive business information and the interests of other stakeholders, the NCP should work with the submitting party to redact any sensitive content in order to facilitate sharing. As much as possible, NCPs should avoid basing fundamental aspects of their decisions on information that is not available to both parties.

49. With respect to communication with the public or third parties about the specific instance, consistent with the core effectiveness criterion of transparency, the parties and the NCP may communicate publicly on the existence of the specific instance, except where otherwise agreed between the parties and the NCP. Furthermore, NCPs are encouraged to allow the parties to communicate publicly about the stage of the process as described in Section I.C.1.-5 of the Procedures (or to do so themselves), and to allow parties to publish their own initial submission. Both parties may also discuss information or documents shared by the other party with their advisors to the specific instance, provided these advisors do not themselves further disclose such information. Other information will be confidential unless otherwise agreed by the parties. In particular, NCPs will inform parties at the outset of the process that they may not disclose at any time facts and arguments shared during the proceedings by the other party or by the NCP itself (including where relevant an external mediator or conciliator) that is not already in the public domain without the consent of the other party or the NCP respectively. In the interest of predictability, trust and confidence, NCPs may seek written assurances from the parties and their advisors in this regard, and adopt provisions in their case-handling procedures that encourage compliance with their non-disclosure requests.

Issues Arising in Non-Adherents

50. As noted in paragraph 2 of the Concepts and Principles chapter, enterprises are encouraged to observe the *Guidelines* wherever they operate, taking into account the particular circumstances of each host country.

- In the event that *Guidelines*-related issues arise in a non-Adherent, home NCPs will take steps to develop an understanding of the issues involved. While it may not always be practicable to obtain access to all pertinent information, or to bring all the parties involved together, the NCP may still be in a position to pursue enquiries and engage in other fact finding activities. Examples of such steps could include contacting the management of the enterprise in the home country, and, as appropriate, embassies and government officials in the non-Adherent.

- Conflicts with host country laws, regulations, rules and policies may make effective implementation of the *Guidelines* in specific instances more difficult than in Adherents. As noted in the commentary to the General Policies chapter, while the *Guidelines* extend beyond the law in many cases, they should not and are not intended to place an enterprise in a situation where it faces conflicting requirements.
- The parties involved will have to be advised of the limitations inherent in implementing the *Guidelines* in non-Adherents.
- Issues relating to the *Guidelines* in non-Adherents could also be discussed at NCP meetings with a view to building expertise in handling issues arising in non-Adherents.

Indicative Timeframe

51. The specific instance procedure comprises five different stages:

1. *Coordination*: Where relevant, coordinate with other NCPs based on the characteristics of the Specific Instance received to determine the lead NCP. Initial coordination arrangements to identify the lead and supporting NCPs should be completed within two months.
2. *Initial assessment and decision whether to offer good offices to assist the parties*: NCPs should seek to conclude an initial assessment within three months after the identification of the lead and supporting NCPs, although additional time might be needed in order to collect or translate information necessary for an informed decision.
3. *Assistance to the parties in their efforts to resolve the issues raised*: If an NCP decides to offer its good offices, it should strive to facilitate the resolution of the issues in a timely manner. Recognising that progress through good offices, including mediation and conciliation, ultimately depends upon the parties involved, the NCP should, after consultation with the parties, establish a reasonable timeframe for the discussion between the parties to resolve the issues raised. If they fail to reach an agreement within this timeframe, the NCP should consult with the parties on the value of continuing its assistance to the parties; if the NCP comes to the conclusion that the continuation of the procedure is not likely to be productive, it should conclude the process and proceed to prepare a statement.
4. *Conclusion of the proceedings:* The NCP should strive to issue its statement within three months after the conclusion of the procedure.
5. *Follow-up*: The NCP may determine its own timetable for any follow-up in consultation with the parties.

52. As a general principle, NCPs should strive to conclude the procedure within 12 months (14 months if coordination to determine a lead NCP is needed) from receipt of the specific instance to its conclusion. It is recognised that this timeframe may need to be extended if circumstances warrant. Such situations include, but are not limited to, situations when the issues arise in a non-Adherent, when the specific instance involves multiple enterprises, multiple submitters and multiple NCPs, or when translations are necessary. Whenever delays are to be expected or experienced in the handling of a specific instance, the NCP should keep the parties informed in a timely manner, so that the proceedings remain predictable. The NCP, in keeping with its case-handling procedures, may decide to issue public updates on the status of cases.

Reporting to the WPRBC and the Investment Committee

53. Reporting is an important responsibility of NCPs that would also help to build up a knowledge base and core competencies in furthering the effectiveness of the *Guidelines*. In this light, NCPs will submit their annual report to the WPRBC and the Investment Committee in order to include in the Annual Report on the OECD Guidelines information on all specific instances that have been initiated by parties. The WPRBC will provide the Committee with an analysis of NCP annual reports to include in the Annual Report on the Guidelines. NCP annual reports should include specific instances in Coordination, Initial Assessment, Good offices, Conclusion or Follow-up. In reporting on implementation activities in specific instances, NCPs will comply with transparency and confidentiality considerations as set out in paragraph I.C-6-7 of the Procedures and in their case-handling procedures.

Support for government efforts to promote responsible business conduct

54. The Decision recognises the support NCPs can provide in the development, administration and coherence of government policies and programmes that promote responsible business conduct, where appropriate and in agreement with relevant government agencies. In particular, NCPs can support the alignment of any such efforts with the *Guidelines* and contribute to maintaining their position as an international standard for responsible business conduct, as well as other OECD instruments and guidance deriving from the *Guidelines*, such as the OECD due diligence guidance.

55. There are various ways in which NCPs may support their government in its efforts to develop, implement and foster coherence of policies to promote responsible business conduct, depending on context. First, NCPs are encouraged to inform relevant government agencies by sharing their statements and reports, as well as other data, surveys and insights, when they are known by the NCP to be relevant to a specific agency's policies and programmes, such as trade advocacy, economic diplomacy, or other support and services to enterprises. Second, Adherents have found it useful to involve their NCP in developing and implementing policies or programmes such as national action plans on responsible business conduct and/or business and human rights. This provision does not change the voluntary nature of the *Guidelines*, and any support provided by or requested from the NCP should take into account its capacities and priorities, and should not detract from its ability to fulfil its responsibilities described in the Decision and the Procedures.

II. Commentary on the Procedures for the Investment Committee, the WPRBC and the Secretariat

56. The Procedures to the Council Decision provides additional guidance to the Committee, the WPRBC and the Secretariat in carrying out their responsibilities, including:

- Discharging their responsibilities in an efficient and timely manner.
- Considering requests from NCPs for assistance, including by providing clarifications, guidance and information on the interpretation of the *Guidelines* in specific instances.
- Holding exchanges of views on the activities of NCPs.
- Providing for the possibility of seeking advice from international partners and experts.

57. The non-binding nature of the *Guidelines* precludes the Committee from acting as a judicial or quasi-judicial body. Nor should the findings and statements made by the NCP (other than interpretations of the *Guidelines*) be questioned by a referral to the Committee. The provision that the Committee shall not reach conclusions on the conduct of individual enterprises has been maintained in the Decision itself.

58. The Secretariat and the WPRBC will consider requests from NCPs for assistance in the event of doubt about the interpretation of the Guidelines in ongoing specific instances. In such situations, NCPs should first contact the Secretariat for information regarding interpretation of the *Guidelines* in similar

cases. Where such information is not available or insufficient to assist the NCP, or the Secretariat is not in a position to assist the NCP, the NCP may seek the guidance of the WPRBC. Such requests will be handled confidentially and, subject to available resources, expeditiously. To expedite the treatment of requests for guidance, the WPRBC may organise *ad hoc* meetings or establish a sub-group to respond to such requests. In such case, the WPRBC will develop procedures to be followed by the sub-group. The information provided by the Secretariat and the guidance of the WPRBC are confidential, case-specific and advisory. The Secretariat will report regularly to the WPRBC, and the WPRBC will report regularly to the Committee, on issues that gave rise to requests for information and guidance, and on responses provided, with due regard for confidentiality. If the WPRBC considers that a question on which guidance is sought requires a clarification of the interpretation of the *Guidelines*, it will invite the NCP to seek a clarification from the Committee on the basis of Section II.2.c) of the Procedures.

59. Clarifications of the interpretation of the *Guidelines* under Section II.2.c) of the Procedures, remain a key responsibility of the Committee to ensure that the interpretation of the *Guidelines* would not vary from country to country. A request for clarification may be filed by an Adherent, an advisory body (BIAC or TUAC) or OECD Watch, including with respect to whether an NCP has correctly interpreted the *Guidelines* or a previous Committee in a closed specific instance. The Committee's clarification will be prepared by the WPRBC with the support of the Secretariat, in accordance with procedures to be defined by the Committee, and be made public on the OECD's website. The Investment Committee will not reach conclusions on the conduct of individual enterprises in issuing its clarification, and NCPs are not expected to re-open a specific instance as a result of a clarification.

60. When discussing NCP activities, the Committee may make recommendations, as necessary, to improve their functioning, including with respect to the effective implementation of the *Guidelines* and to address any situation in which an NCP becomes non-functioning. In particular, the Committee may determine, based on an NCP's last two annual reporting cycles and upon a proposal by the WPRBC, that an NCP has, for an extended period of time and without legitimate reason, manifestly not been operating in a way consistent with the Procedures. Such a finding may rest on, for example, the repeated failure to assign the resources required for the basic discharge of NCP responsibilities, demonstrably inadequate institutional arrangements, absence of any promotional activities, repeated and significant undue delays in the handling of specific instances, or lack of reporting. The Committee may then make recommendations to the country of the NCP and invite it to report on implementation within a specified timeframe and make further recommendations in case such reporting does not satisfy the Committee that the NCP is functioning in a way consistent with the Procedures. The Committee may request the Secretariat to assist the Adherent in the implementation of the recommendations. The Adherent whose NCP is concerned should participate in the process in good faith and is expected to join consensus except in exceptional circumstances as determined by that country.

61. A substantiated submission by an adhering country, an advisory body (BIAC or TUAC) or OECD Watch that an NCP was not fulfilling its procedural responsibilities in the implementation of the *Guidelines* in specific instances will also be considered by the Committee. The Committee's response will be prepared by the WPRBC with the support of the Secretariat, in accordance with procedures defined by the Committee. It will be approved by consensus. The Adherent whose NCP is the subject of a substantiated submission should participate in the process in good faith and is expected to join consensus except in exceptional circumstances as determined by that country. The Committee will give the Adherent in question the possibility to state its view on the substantiated submission prior to its decision, and the Committee may invite the Adherent to report on the implementation of any recommendations within twelve months of the response.

62. In order to engage with non-Adherents on matters covered by the *Guidelines*, the Committee may invite interested non-Adherents to its meetings, annual Roundtables on Corporate Responsibility, and meetings relating to specific projects on responsible business conduct.

63. Finally, the Committee and the WPRBC may wish to call on experts to address and report on broader issues (for example, child labour or human rights) or individual issues, or to improve the effectiveness of procedures. For this purpose, the Committee could call on OECD in-house expertise, international organisations, the advisory bodies (BIAC and TUAC), OECD Watch, non-governmental organisations, academics and others. It is understood that this may not become a panel to settle individual issues.